KT-214-553

KO SAMUI

ENCOUNTER

CHINA WILLIAMS

Ko Samui Encounter

Published by Lonely Planet Publications Pty Ltd
ABN 36 005 607 983

Australia	Head Office, Locked Bag 1, Footscray, Vic 3011 ☎ 03 8379 8000 fax 03 8379 8111 talk2us@lonelyplanet.com.au
USA	150 Linden St, Oakland, CA 94607 ☎ 510 250 6400 toll free 800 275 8555 fax 510 893 8572 info@lonelyplanet.com
UK	Media Centre, 201 Wood Lane, London W12 7TQ ☎ 020 8433 1333, fax 020 8702 0112

This title was commissioned in Lonely Planet's Melbourne office and produced by: **Commissioning Editor** Carolyn Boicos **Coordinating Editor** Victoria Harrison **Coordinating Cartographer** Barbara Benson **Layout Designer** Carol Jackson **Managing Editors** Sasha Baskett, Helen Christinis, Melanie Dankel **Managing Cartographer** David Connolly **Cover Designer** Pepi Bluck **Series Designers** Mik Ruff, Wendy Wright **Project Managers** Rachel Imeson, Glenn van der Knijff **Managing Layout Designer** Celia Wood **Thanks to** Glenn Beanland, Stefanie Di Trocchio, Bruce Evans, Ryan Evans, Justin Flynn, Quentin Frayne, Jim Hsu, Paul Iacono, Laura Jane, Charity Mackinnon, Adam McCrow, Naomi Parker, Gerard Walker

Cover photograph Ko Samui, Thailand, ocean fishing, Art Directors. **Internal photographs** p4 © Roger Cracknell p22/Thailand / Alamy; p6 © Tibor Bognar / Alamy; p23 © Peter Treanor / Alamy; p95 © Jon Arnold Images Ltd / Alamy. All other photographs by Lonely Planet Images, and by Austin Bush except p22 Dennis Johnson; p98 Kristin Piljay; p101 Richard Nebesky.

All images are copyright of the photographers unless otherwise indicated. Many of the images in this guide are available for licensing from **Lonely Planet Images:** www.lonelyplanetimages.com.

ISBN 9781741794274

10 9 8 7 6 5 4 3

Printed by 1010 Printing International, Hong Kong. Printed in China.

HOW TO USE THIS BOOK
Colour-Coding & Maps
Colour-coding is used for symbols on maps and in the text that they relate to (eg all eating venues on the maps and in the text are given a green knife and fork symbol). Each neighbourhood also gets its own colour, and this is used down the edge of the page and throughout that neighbourhood section.

Prices
Multiple prices listed with reviews (eg €10/5 or €10/5/20) indicate adult/child, adult/concession or adult/child/family.

Send us your feedback We love to hear from readers — your comments help make our books better. We read every word you send us, and we always guarantee that your feedback goes straight to the appropriate authors. The most useful submissions are rewarded with a free book. To send us your updates and find out about Lonely Planet events, newsletters and travel news visit our award-winning website: **www.lonelyplanet.com/contact**.

Note: We may edit, reproduce and incorporate your comments in Lonely Planet products such as guidebooks, websites and digital products, so let us know if you don't want your comments reproduced or your name acknowledged. For a copy of our privacy policy visit **www.lonelyplanet.com/privacy**.

CHINA WILLIAMS

China thought her commuting days to Thailand were over after she had a baby, but Samui proved to be the perfect merging of work and family. She dusted off her backpack, got a passport for her one-year old son and introduced him to Thailand, the family's distant 'backyard'. He took his first steps in a Mae Nam guesthouse and learned to wave at every vendor.

China first came to Thailand nearly 10 years ago to teach English in Isan and started returning years later to write Lonely Planet books mainly to Bangkok. This was her second, but most charmed, visit to Samui where she discovered that good food can occur on the islands. She lives with her husband, Matt, and son, Felix, in the leafy suburb of Takoma Park, Maryland (US).

Additional material was provided for this edition by Brandon Presser.

CHINA'S THANKS

Thanks to super nanny and research assistant Stacey McCarthy. Mama's pride to Felix for loving Thailand as much as I do. Additional thanks to Somchai, Pariya, Nittiphong, Saithip, Shelley, Nong and the staff at Bhundari. More thanks to Carolyn Boicos and the production team at Lonely Planet. And to my husband, Matt, for surviving without us and being our airport chauffeur. More thanks to my domestic super nannies: Mary, Mandy and Kathleen.

THE PHOTOGRAPHER

After working several years at a stable job, Austin Bush made the questionable decision to pursue a career as a freelance photographer. This choice has since taken him as far as Pakistan's Karakoram Hwy and as near as Bangkok's Or Tor Kor Market. For samples of his work, see www.austinbushphotography.com.

Our readers Many thanks to the travellers who wrote to us with helpful hints, useful advice and interesting anecdotes. Bianca Barbaro, Kathy Belpaeme, Jason Brown, Pablo Contestabile, Bryan Cronk, Brent Kendall, Tracey Seslen, Melanie Simunovic, Mark Westerfield.

Souvenir dolls

CONTENTS

Our authors are independent, dedicated travellers. They don't research using just the internet or phone, and they don't take freebies, so you can rely on their advice being well researched and impartial. They travel widely visiting thousands of places, taking great pride in getting all the details right and telling it how it is.

THIS IS KO SAMUI

Synonymous with sun and fun, Samui is a bouillon cube of tropical paradise and modern convenience. Even though it's a small city by the sea, the island wears a soft stole of white sand beaches, which are some of Thailand's leggiest and most legendary.

The blue topaz waters heave and retreat in a rhythmic sequence and the coconut palms bow in agreement that you have indeed arrived in paradise. The path to such an idyll is antithetically easy; the flight from Bangkok hardly imposes on the day's itinerary. And the sun shines bright, eager to polish its worshippers into the colour of burnished gold.

Despite its long slumber through history, Samui has wholly embraced the present and packages all the mod cons for its parade of visitors. City distractions, like shopping, eating and partying, are right on the doorstep to the beach. International-style resorts have more comforts and better housekeepers than at home. And the camaraderie of holiday crowds infuses Chaweng, Samui's busiest beach, with a celebratory mood. Leftovers from the backwater backpacker days might sniff that Samui is overly commercial, others are pleased to find it so civilised.

The beaches are so diverse you'd have to island-hop for months to find equivalents. Yet here on Phuket's younger sister are the matches to each traveller's personal beach ideal. Bo Phut and the commercial area of Fisherman's Village are urbane and mannered. Mae Nam satisfies the Thailand-philes with morning markets, shanty food shacks and Thai life powered by a motorcycle. And the south coast is still asleep under a coconut tree, hardly aware that the 21st century has moved in next door.

Samui is so adaptable that its fans span the travelling categories: fortnighters, honeymooners and families, united in their love of sand and sea. The newest arrivals are health tourists lured by wellness centres that concoct rejuvenating tonics of fasting, yoga and ocean breezes.

Top Ko Samui's spirit houses (p120) are an animistic tradition, built on pedestals. **Bottom** Chaweng Noi (p41) is one of the most peaceful beaches on the island.

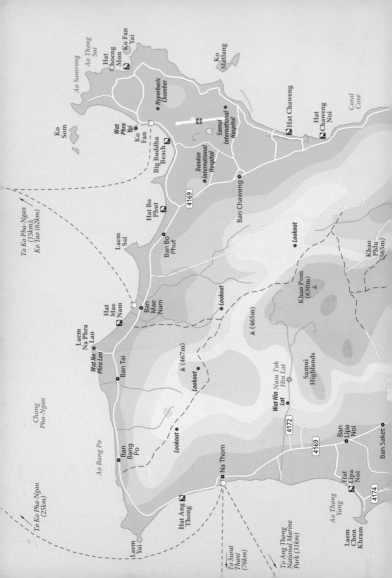

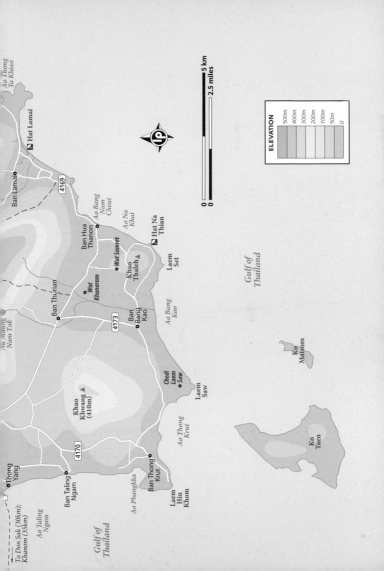

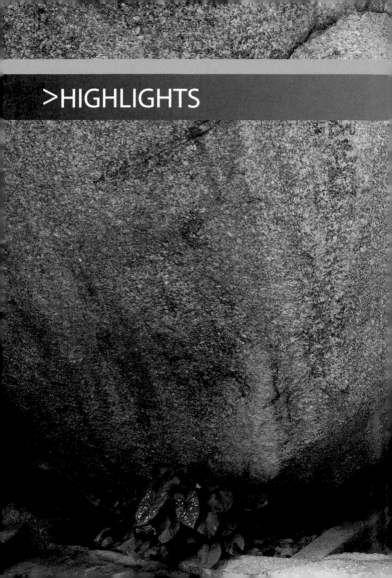

>HIGHLIGHTS

Pamper your body at Tamarind Springs (p19)

>1 SAMUI FOOD SHOPS

FEASTING ON COCONUT ISLAND

To thwart your best bikini intentions, Samui is a smorgasbord of fabulous food, from basic Thai standards to fiery regional curries as well as the fruits of the sea. With contributions from northeastern Thailand and northern Europe, Samui has become a melting pot of culinary cultures but its home-grown dishes still survive in humble huts and sprawling seafood shacks.

Influenced by the mainland, Samui is peppered with *kôw gaang* (rice and curry) shops, usually just a wooden shack displaying large metal pots of southern Thai-style curries. Folks pull up on their motorcycles, lift up the lids to survey the vibrantly coloured contents, and pick one for lunch. *Kôw gaang* shops are easily found along the Ring Rd (Rd 4169) and sell out of the good stuff by 1pm.

Any build up of local motorcycles is usually a sign of a good meal in progress. The day and evening markets feed most Thais most of the time. Ask a local about their favourite restaurant and they just shrug, but ask them about the markets and they'll talk until both of

you are starving. Laem Din Market (p46) has a busy food centre that feeds the masses until 2am. Lamai Day Market (p59) has a mix of takeaway meals and vendor snacks throughout the day. Hua Thanon Market (p71) is best visited in the morning to explore Thailand's peculiar breakfast rituals. Na Thon Night Market (p77) is rarely visited by tourists but it has a batch of local wok varieties as well as affordable sunset views.

You'll soon discover that the tastiest meals come from restaurants that are short on décor. The famous seafood restaurants, for example, are little more than open-air barns squatting on the sand beside the ocean, which generously donates scenery and seafood to the evening meal. Bang Po Seafood (p83) and Sabeinglae (p61) are two preservers of old-fashioned Samui food. Coconut, both the milk and the flesh, is often the building block of Samui-specific dishes. Sea urchins, local octopus, seaweed and other less glamorous ingredients are combined with spectacular success. You might not be able to identify the components but the flavours are pleasingly pungent.

For a guide to specific dishes, see Food (p115).

>2 AROUND THE ISLAND
CRUISING FOR CURRY AND COCONUT

As soon as you step onto the island, the tour brainwashing begins and you'll be papered with brochures promising action, adventure and trips around the island. First, the typical tour only travels around a small corner of the southeast of the island and rarely comes close to circumnavigating Samui. Second, most companies include a slew of depressing, county fair–style animal shows that will make you want to become an animal-rights activist. Instead we recommend doing the island at your own pace, either by hiring a car or motor-cycle for the day, or chartering a taxi for four or five hours (2000B).

Traffic along the eastern section of Rd 4169, better known as the Ring Rd, is reminiscent of Bangkok but the commuting rush doesn't start until the lazy hour of 10am and congestion diminishes south of Lamai. Start the day early with a wake-up call at Hin Ta Hin Yai (p56), Lamai's famously aroused rock formations. Then catch the morn-

ing activity at the fishing village of Ban Hua Thanon (p66) and Hua Thanon Market (p71). If kids are part of the pack, treat them to an elephant ride at one of the inland waterfalls (p69) and a visit to the Samui Butterfly Garden (p68). For the grown-ups, factor in a massage and herbal steam bath at Kamalaya Koh Samui (p69).

Then drop off the Ring Rd onto the coconut trail of Rd 4170, which travels along the sleepy south coast. At any point, pull over and have lunch if you spot a table lined with metal bowls: this is the island's ubiquitous *kôw gaang* shops.

Dive deeper into the coconut trees with a detour to Chedi Laem Saw (p66), perched on a lonely point of land. If an hour or two has passed, you'll need to eat again, lest you dishonour the Thai tradition of snacking throughout the day. Cruise over to a waterfront restaurant in Thong Krut to survey the shallow harbour. Then loop back to the Ring Rd in time for a quick dip, back at the hotel pool, before dinner.

>3 HEALTH RETREATS & DETOX PROGRAMS

TAKING THE CURE

People come to Samui to look good: they want to get a tan, get skinny and feel fabulous. And the twin demands of health and beauty have inspired a hybrid industry of spa pampering with health regimens, like cleansing fasts and yoga. This is the modern version of Roman baths or Victorian-era hill stations. Taking the cure on Samui can range from a seven-day fast to a one-hour meditation class. Most of the health centres are flexible since people often leave home with good intentions and then ultimately realise they are on holiday.

So what does the cure entail? Instead of baking on a beach chair, fasters wake up with the sun for an itinerary of detox drinks, coffee enemas, broth soups and nutritional supplements. Yum. But abstinence is rewarded with massage, yoga, herbal steam treatments and other relaxation techniques to create a day-long meditative state. When the period ends, the fast is broken with Thailand's fabulous array of tropical fruit and fruit juices, such as coconut, pineapple and papaya. Most fasting veterans recommend taking a week to indulge (this is Thailand – a culinary superstar – after all) and then a week of purification.

Spa Samui (p56) started the fasting trend on the island and is still one of the most affordable detox programs around. The resort facilities are rustic, and oversight of fasters is minimal. You get out what you put in – in more than one way. Equally free-form, Absolute Yoga studio (p85) in Bo Phut doles out detox drinks and supplements to the cleansing curious. Folks start the day with yoga classes and then chase it with the required juices and shoot the breeze before wandering off to the beach.

At the opposite end of the scale, Dharma Healing International (p78) was established by a former student of Wat Suan Mok, the famous meditation temple in Chaiya, and incorporates a devoutly spiritual aspect into its cleansing program. This is the most intensive and personalised program on the island.

For a resort escape, Kamalaya Koh Samui (p69) relaxes with its picture-perfect setting and then entertains with its New Age treatments. Health Oasis Resort (p82) differs with its impressive array of alternative medicine treatments and its far-from-temptation location.

>4 CHAWENG

GETTING TOASTED WITH SAMUI'S VIVACIOUS BLONDE

Lather up the limbs for a visit to Samui's number one beach: mighty Chaweng (p36). Though once a backpacker secret, Chaweng is now an international celebrity drawing in the young ones on a beach-and-binge tour and the older ones spicing up life beyond the suburbs. It is busy and crowded – more of a beach amusement park than a beach getaway – but it is still stunning, despite the topless European grandmas.

During the heat of the day, the beach is filled to the rim with sun-bathers and swimmers, creating an ambient roar of excitement. As evening approaches, the beach changes into its indigo night clothes and the beachfront restaurants light lanterns as invitations to roaming appetites. Beachside barbecues serve a heaped helping of freshly caught seafood and ocean-side scenery.

Heading inland from the beach leads to busy Chaweng Beach Rd, a less-than-marvellous stretch of asphalt filled with traffic, souvenir shops and tacky neon – an assaulting reminder that this is Asia. But the commercial chaos fuels the carnival ambiance that has earned Chaweng its second accolade as a party animal. Bars and clubs on Soi Green Mango and Soi Solo mix international music with local beverages for a global good time. And then there are the bucket drinks – a mad scientist's mixture of booze served in plastic buckets – that turn adult beverages into kid's play.

>5 TAMARIND SPRINGS

STEEPING IN THE NATURAL ELEMENTS AT A JUNGLE SPA

Way off in Laos, rural temples maintain makeshift herbal steam rooms, or more accurately, steam closets, where the therapeutic herbs and pastoral setting achieve an even deeper sense of relaxation than the laid-back land can on its own. It was this modest 'spa' experience that inspired Shelley Poplak to create Tamarind Springs (p57), a merging of the natural landscape with traditional bathing therapies, massage and the new generation of spa treatments. Tamarind Spring's setting is serene, tucked into a hill-side surrounded by the fanlike canopy of coconut trees. The sounds of the forest 'breathing' – chirping insects and rustling leaves – invites visitors to follow their own breath, the fundamental component of meditation. A deliberate walk up a small rise leads to the first station: a steam room and plunge pool sheltered by sculpted, balloon-shaped boulders that balance on tapered points. Guests can steam and plunge for an hour or more before ascending to the final station: the massage *säh·lah* (often written as 'sala'; open pavilion) overlooking the tree tops. The newly added Forest Spa offers the same natural ambience with the added benefit of private massage rooms and a more dramatic bathing area. Afterwards, savour this state at the café before re-entering sweaty Samui.

HIGHLIGHTS

>6 FISHERMAN'S VILLAGE
FISHING FOR DINNER WITH THE BOURGEOIS BOHEMIAN

Bo Phut's fantastic, Fisherman's Village (p84) is a rising star in the Samui constellation. More reserved than Chaweng, more cultured than Lamai, it is the new best friend for the well-dressed and the well-heeled counterculturalists who travel with a bag of urban sophistication, a strong currency and a stamp-filled passport. At dinnertime, the village is romantically lit with lanterns and dainty restaurants. Patrons stroll about the place, showing off their sun-kissed skin, and hardly a motorcycle or taxi muscles its way into the pedestrian parade. Though there are a few hobby businesses, thanks to the European empty-nesters, many of the international restaurants are more committed to the palate than the usual Western cuisine restaurants that coast on a revolving door of tourists. To match the clientele's expectations, the restaurants dress themselves in chic décor to compete for the globally savvy diners. Come for dinner and imagine yourself as an accomplished dot-commie or other new-media tycoon.

>7 ANG THONG NATIONAL PARK

EXPLORING DESERTED ISLANDS

After an hour's boat journey from Samui, you start to see a looming landmass on the horizon. Slipping closer, the jumbled shadow begins to separate into distinct islands, seemingly moored together in a far-flung marina. Pockmarked limestone outcroppings bow towards the sea like ship masts and the illusion of self-motion make the anchored shapes appear to bob in the sapphire-coloured water. Closer still and the archipelago reveals its internal geometry: a watery maze between tight-knit primordial figures.

Designated a park in 1980, Ang Thong National Park (Golden Bowl) is a collection of 40 (some sources say 42) islands, 35km west of Samui, a boat journey of two hours. Some of the rugged islands are fringed with golden beaches and are mainly devoid of human inhabitants, except for the daily migration of tourists from Samui, overnighters at the park-operated bungalows, and a few local fisherfolk. The powerful ocean has whittled away at the malleable limestone to create dramatic arches, hidden caves and lagoons inside of the islands. This dynamic and mysterious landscape hosted the fictionalised commune in the other backpacker bible, *The Beach*, by Alex Garland.

Most visitors come on day trips from Samui to kayak between the islands and snorkel around the sheltered coves. For more information on Ang Thong, see p96.

>8 KO TAO

SWIMMING WITH THE FISHES

The Gulf of Thailand is a wide, shallow basin that has cultivated a diverse underwater community of marine life amid a landscape of submerged pinnacles and gently sloping reefs. The best diving is near Ko Tao (p101), 65km from Samui.

Of the underwater spectacles, Chumphon Pinnacles is considered a world-class dive site with four towering pinnacles blanketed in pink anemones. Southwest Pinnacles has colourful soft coral and schools of fish. A little closer to Samui (32km away), Sail Rock is known for its wall dives, underwater chimney and whale sharks.

If you'd rather stick closer to the surface, strap on a mask and fins and wade out from Ko Tao's beaches. Laem Thian is the spot for small sharks, Ao Hin Wong has crystal-clear waters, and Ao Mamuang has staghorns and table coral easily accessible for beginners.

Most dive companies happily shuttle people from Samui to Ko Tao's dive sites, but it is a two-hour journey each way, a demanding commute for folks hoping to get away from one. To save fuel, money and time, base yourself in Ko Tao, where dive shops and certification courses are cheap and plentiful. Dive prices are standardised and start at 9800B for a PADI open-water certification.

Conditions are best from July to October when the seas are calm and visibility is high, but some sites have their own micro-climates independent of the season and ocean temperament.

>KO SAMUI DIARY

Since Samui makes its living from being on vacation, nearly every day is a holiday. But island-wide, Samui looks to the national Buddhist holidays and a few home-grown events to come together. Other social engagements include the monthly rotation of dance parties (see the boxed text, p51) in Samui and on nearby Ko Pha-Ngan. The international holidays, like Christmas, Easter and Valentine's Day, get promoted by the hotels and restaurants with special arrangements. Government offices and banks in Na Thon close for national holidays but the beach businesses typically cater to the needs of the tourists.

Celebrate hard on New Year's Eve (p26)

KO SAMUI DIARY

FEBRUARY

Chinese New Year
Samui has a large population of ethnic Chinese, who honour their cultural lunar new year with family dinners, fireworks and religious blessings. Outside of Na Thon, this holiday is more obvious by the surge in tourists from Singapore and Hong Kong. This is a lunar holiday and sometimes it occurs in March.

APRIL

Songkran
Thais welcome in their lunar new year with a water-throwing celebration. It used to be a gentle dousing but has evolved into a full drenching. Samui's Songkran isn't as wet and wild as Bangkok's and Chiang Mai's, but there are some bucket brigades that keep the traffic police soaked. Other events include hotel parties, beauty pageants and the Muslim tradition of buffalo fighting. This holiday is celebrated from 13 to 15 April.

MAY

Visakha Bucha
Buddha's triumvirate milestones (his birth, enlightenment and death) are celebrated at temples throughout the island. Merit-makers go to the temples to listen to sermons and hold candlelit processions around the main chapel. This is a lunar holiday so dates vary.

JUNE

Koh Samui Regatta
www.samuiregatta.com
Elegant sail boats from around the world harness the wind and slice the waves in this five-day race around the island. You can spot the cruisers from the beach at Mae Nam or applaud the race teams at the opening and closing ceremonies, which are open to the public. One veteran of the seas is the *Somtam Express*, a boat specifically designed for Southeast Asian waters.

SINGING BIRDS & FIGHTING BUFFALO
For a laid-back island, competition is a popular pastime. Local Samui people enjoy raising and training singing birds to compete in bird-song contests. Usually known as compliant creatures, the water buffalo gets to push around more than a plough when two males are matched up in the fighting buffalo contests. Na Thon's Tourist Authority of Thailand (TAT) office (see p136) and taxi drivers can find out the dates and locations of these events.

Listen to the cacophony of a songbird singing competition (p24)

JULY

Khao Phansa

The beginning of the rainy season is the start of the Buddhist Lent when young men traditionally enter the monastery. This is a lunar holiday, so dates vary.

AUGUST

Samui Food & Product Fair

Sample some of Samui's culinary creations at this two-day celebration. The first day features free tastings of Samui-grown fruits, dishes from hotel restaurants and vendor specialities. The second day includes cultural dancing displays and Thai-style fanfare. Host sites vary each year.

SEPTEMBER

International Reef Clean-Up Day

Project AWARE, the environmental foundation of the dive industry, organises this international event that relies on volunteers to pick-up rubbish off the reefs and beaches. Samui's dive shops offer discounted rates to divers who want to participate in picking-up refuse.

KO SAMUI DIARY

Gaze up at the 12m-high Big Buddha statue at Wat Phra Yai (p93)

NOVEMBER

Chakphra Festival

A southern Thai tradition, Chakphra commemorates Buddha's return to earth with a procession of a Buddha statue through the streets or waterways. In Samui, Chakphra is celebrated in Na Thon town and in Ko Pha-Ngan (where the festival is orchestrated on the sea). Traditional music, including drum-beating contests, and dancing usually follow. This is a lunar holiday, marking the end of the rainy season and the end of Buddhist Lent (Ork Phansa) – dates vary.

Loy Kratong

This religious festival honouring the goddess of water is celebrated in Samui at Wat Phra Yai (Big Buddha Temple), at the ferry jetties in Na Thon and at Chaweng Lake in Chaweng. After the floating of the ceremonial boats, there are parties featuring Thai singers well known in southern Thailand. This is a lunar holiday and sometimes falls in October.

DECEMBER

New Year's Eve

Chaweng is the place to be to bid adieu to the old year. Hotels host firework displays, drink specials and DJ parties. Gecko Village (p92) features London DJs.

It may not be the safest option, but motorcycle travel (p132) is quick and convenient

ITINERARIES

Heaven forbid you'll grow bored just lazing on the beach. But if your book becomes tiresome and your skin sufficiently bronzed then remind yourself that you're in a foreign country with day trips around the island or multiday trips to nearby islands. There are indeed patches of sand other than the one between your toes and the interior is filled with mountainous terrain and hill-top vistas. Samui is fairly easy to get around with private transport, though the roads are little more than village lanes with urbanised traffic.

THREE DAYS

If you're coming to Samui for a long weekend, partake in the bare necessities: sunbathing, snacking, shopping and spa-ing. Claim a beach chair in Chaweng (p36) if you want city distractions with some natural beauty. The next day, go on an 'Around the Island' tour (p14) or cruise up to Fisherman's Village (p84) for dinner. Spend your last day sitting in the steam cave at Tamarind Springs (p19), Spa Samui Village (p57) or Kamalaya Koh Samui (p69) or spa away the day at Hideaway Spa (p94) or Anantara Spa (p87).

FIVE DAYS

With close to a week, you can set sail on a day trip to Ang Thong National Park (p96). Or spend the day beach-hopping on the north (p80) and west (p72) coasts. Climb up the hill for evening drinks at Q Bar Samui (p52) or devote your Wednesday night to Ark Bar (p49) and its Ibiza-style beach parties. Keep an eye out for one of the monthly dance parties held at Chaweng Lake View (see the boxed text, p51).

TWO WEEKS

With a second week, you'll have time to explore Samui's sister islands: Ko Tao (p101) and Ko Pha-Ngan (p98). After a week above the water, spend the remainder below the surface on a dive tour. Dive trips leave from Samui or you can save time and energy by basing yourself on Ko Tao. If

---

Top left Vegetable stall at Laem Din Market (p47) **Top right** Sun lounges on Hat Chaweng (p41) **Bottom** Thai-cooking class at Samui Institute of Thai Culinary Arts (p42).

Samui's version of urban-meets-beach is too much for you, hang your hammock on one of the laid-back beaches of Ko Pha-Ngan, an old pal to the backpacking bohemians.

HEALTHY SAMUI

Health nuts flock to Samui for the new millennium's version of R&R: health retreats and detox programs (p16). Most programs last seven days but a few can be abbreviated to 3½ days. Between skipping meals is a busy day of yoga, massage and herbal steam baths. Alternatively, you can skip the fast and go for the class (meditation, yoga, raw-food cooking). Many fasters build in a week of beach holiday before their health regimen starts.

WITH THE FAMILY

Once the kids turn to prunes after days of swimming in the ocean and the pool, set off on some land adventures. Explore Samui's jungle interior on a zip-line with Canopy Adventures (p41) or as a saddle king aboard an elephant on one of the Waterfall Jungle Treks (p69). Chase butterflies at the Samui Butterfly Garden (p68) and spot a mummified monk at Wat Khunaram (p68). Cultivate little foodies with tours of the day market in Na Thon (p77) and Chaweng's Laem Din Market (p47). And urge the kids

FORWARD PLANNING

Only during the wettest months of October and November does Samui experience a low season for tourism. The rest of the year is split between high season and peak season and reservations for accommodation should be made as far in advance as possible. Once you arrive, you can book restaurants, tours and onward travel to nearby islands with local travel agents.

A month before you go Book your hotel and your connecting flight from Bangkok. Bangkok Airways has discount tickets for the first and last flights of the day that sell out quickly. If the cheap seats are gone, check back in a week. Be sure to reserve your spot if you're coming for a health retreat; Spa Samui fills up quickly.

One week before you go Make reservations for dive trips and overnight accommodation in Bangkok if you've got a layover. Book spa treatments now if you're visiting during international holidays. Make sure you can still wear your bathing suit from last summer. Stock up on reading material for the flight and for lazing on the beach.

The day before you go Relax, soon you'll be on holiday.

towards enlightenment with a visit to Wat Phra Yai (Big Buddha Temple; p93).

HONEYMOON SAMUI

After the 'I dos', hide away with your spouse at one of Samui's self-contained luxury hotels or go more boho at a boutique hotel. Dine with the stars and gastronomy at Zazen Restaurant (p91) or Dining on the Rocks (p94). Toast the view at the Cliff Bar & Grill (p58). All Samui spas have honeymoon and couples packages, should you need double relaxation. And explore the quieter west coast (p72) for uninterrupted strolls hand-in-hand. Try out a cooking course at Samui Institute of Thai Culinary Arts (p42) because the couple that cooks together stays together.

The peaceful fishing village of Thong Krut (p64) is used as a launching pad for day trips to nearby islands

BEACHES & TOWNS

Equal parts city and country, Samui has developed primarily along the coast, with the mountainous interior dominated by coconut plantations. Each coast reflects a different personality based on the quality of its beach and the temperament of its residents.

The east coast has the most spectacular beaches: long and curvaceous, and pinned at the extremities by forested headlands. The sand is soft on tender, winter-sheltered feet and the sea is an iridescent blue-green that crashes ashore leaving behind a foamy moustache. The commercial areas of Chaweng and Lamai are busy and cacophonous, built in a hurry and without flourish. The around-the-island highway, known as the Ring Rd (or Rd 4169), is as congested as a head cold on this coast, challenging the R&R that most visitors dreamed of.

Along the south coast are little villages – Ban Thurian, Ban Harn, Ban Tha Po – hardly discernible from each other. A stand of trees, a few traditional wooden houses and sarong-clad ladies busy with chores and children. Road 4170 is an uncrowded ribbon of concrete that loops off of the Ring Rd and meanders through the shade, making for good cruising and even bicycling.

The west coast is quiet and local with adequate beaches well-insulated from the east coast crowds but within easy proximity of Na Thon, the island's administrative centre and a textbook example of a southern Thai town.

For some, the 'golden age' of Samui was 10 years ago when bungalows abutted the beach, tourists intermingled with the local population and locals juggled fishing nets instead of fire batons at techno parties. Well, it is always '10 years ago' somewhere on Samui, and for the moment that's Bang Po and Mae Nam on the north coast. The next cove over is Bo Phut, a favourite of young families, young professionals and more urban types. Beach-hoppers will feel they've discovered paradise once they push into the Choeng Mon and the northeastern cape's parched cliff landscape.

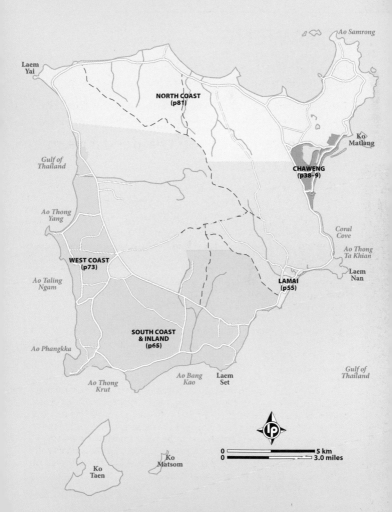

Laem
Yai

NORTH COAST
(p81)

Ao Samrong

Ko
Matlang

Gulf of
Thailand

CHAWENG
(p38–9)

Ao Thong
Yang

Coral
Cove

Ao Thong
Ta Khian

WEST COAST
(p73)

Laem
Nan

Ao Taling
Ngam

LAMAI
(p55)

SOUTH COAST
& INLAND
(p65)

Ao Phangkka

Ao Bang
Kao

Laem
Set

Gulf of
Thailand

Ao Thong
Krut

Ko
Taen

Ko
Matsom

0   5 km
0   3.0 miles

>CHAWENG

Chaweng has the beach version of an hourglass figure: soft white sand that gently curves from Ko Matlang in the north to Chaweng Noi in the south. The wide swath in the centre is crowded. Bodies of various shapes and sizes, in various states of undress, lie prostrate before the tropical sun god, while jet skis skip and roar over the watery contours. Music blares from the beach bars and vendors tirelessly trudge through the sand to deliver amusements to the amusable. The beach is quieter at its extremities though the northern end is rocky and narrow. The southern end has good swimming and fewer visitors to share it with.

The dynamic duo of sun and fun were largely a young person's sport when Samui was known only by backpackers. But today, Chaweng has replaced the cheap bungalows with international-style resorts, popular with families with older children and package tourists. Chaweng's commercial strip is a little Bangkok by the sea that wakes up at noon and parties well into the next day.

CHAWENG

Please see over for map

👁 SEE

The beach, of course, is the number-one thing to see in Chaweng. You can rouse yourself from your sun-induced coma to take a look at a few spots, or just read about them here and return to your slumber.

👁 CHAWENG LAKE
Chaweng Lake Rd
By the light of the harsh daytime sun, Chaweng Lake is an example of everything that is wrong with Samui. The public park is poorly maintained, half constructed and devoid of shade. But come sunset, it springs to life – ordinary Thai life, that is – with aerobics classes in one area, football practice in another and strolling families enjoying the cool breezes. It's a charming glimpse into provincial Thailand.

👁 CHEDI KHAO HUA JOOK
north of Chaweng Lake
Atop Khao Hua Jook (Top-Knot Mountain), this stupa commands powerful views of Chaweng Lake, the beach and beyond. You'll need private transport to reach this area. Take the road that leads to Q Bar and follow the roundabout to the car park; from there you follow the stairs to the summit

👁 DOG RESCUE CENTER SAMUI
☎ 0 7741 3490; www.samuidog.org; Soi 3, Chaweng Beach Rd; ⏱ 9am-6pm
Thai dogs tend to live traditional lives: roaming the sois in packs, raiding garbage piles and losing the battle against mange. It is a life of freedom and suffering, with little intervention from humans.

FIRST BUNGALOW
The resort hotels in Samui might seem like faceless corporations but they are monuments to local family empires. Before tourism arrived, the favourite son or daughter inherited the fertile coconut-growing land in the interior while the other siblings were given the anaemic coastal areas or sent to Bangkok to get a job. Fortunes reversed when the backpackers 'discovered' the island in the mid-1970s and brought with them the commodity of tourism. Claiming to be the first on Chaweng, First Bungalow Beach Resort got its start as a homestay when a local couple met two American travellers on the train and invited them back to their Chaweng Noi home. Word spread and the homestay turned into a bungalow guesthouse charging 20B a night. Fifteen years later, the guesthouse turned into a multistorey hotel and by the late 1990s the primary guests were package tourists. Today First Bungalow is a minicity, and the family has expanded its operations to two other hotels, managed under the Orapin Beach Resort Group, named for the family matriarch.

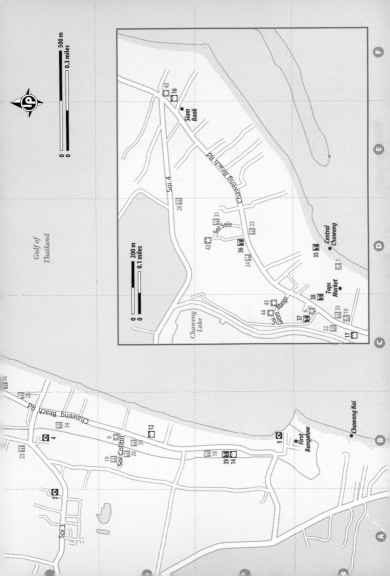

Gulf of
Thailand

500 m
0.3 miles

200 m
0.1 miles

Sol 3

Chaweng Beach Rd

25

3

4

34

Sol Colibri

19

20

30

9

12

17

18

39

14

5

First
Bungalow

Chaweng Noi

Sol 4

26

Chaweng Beach Rd

43

16

Siam
Bank

Chaweng Lake

Sol Green Mango

44

45

37

22

17

Sol Solo

42

36

24

31

23

38

33

10

35

7

Central
Chaweng

Tops
Market

Sawang Srikwan
Retired operator of First Bungalow Beach Resort in Chaweng Beach

What do you do for a living? I grew up in Chaweng and went to work for the US Army in Chonburi. Then I came back and ran a homestay and guesthouse for my parents when the hippie people first started coming to Samui to smoke marijuana. Now I'm an old man and retired. **How did you advertise your guesthouse?** If I saw foreigners I would tell them about Chaweng beach. I made a map so they could come here from the pier and my slogan was 'sea, sand, sun'. **What is special about Samui?** Samui brings happiness to people. I know in America and Europe, you wear an overcoat every season. You need sand and sea to feel good. **How has Chaweng changed over the years?** Chaweng is crowded but it has everything people want. That's why people come here. If there is something you don't like, tell me and I'll make a recommendation to the government.

Back in 1999, two Europeans opened an animal clinic to provide the previously unavailable services of free spaying and medical care to the island's dogs. The centre has since expanded to a larger facility in Taling Ngam and invites volunteers at either location to cuddle, care or adopt the animals. Call for directions.

☪ MUAY THAI STADIUM

☎ 0 7741 3504; cnr Soi Reggae & Laem Din Market Rd; admission1000B

'Tonight only' is the mantra blasted through the loudspeakers of the pick-up trucks that circle Chaweng advertising a *moo·ay tai* (Thai boxing; also spelt *muay thai*) fight most nights. Though the audience is mostly tourists, Chaweng's stadium (south of Chaweng Lake) hosts an increasing number of respected showdowns between title fighters as well as match-ups between foreign and local fighters.

☪ PUBLIC BEACH ACCESS

btwn Hat Chaweng & Chaweng Noi;
🚌 ♿

Locals take their lunch break at the small bamboo *săh·lah* (open pavilion) near the spirit house beside First Bungalow Resort. As beach observers appear so do the food vendors because Thais are always ready for a snack. Local fisherman also congregate here before and

after pulling their colourful long-tail boats into the neighbouring canal.

🏃 DO

🏃 BLUE STAR KAYAKING

☎ 0 7741 3231; www.bluestars.info; Gallery La Fayette, Chaweng Beach Rd; tours 1990B; ⌚ tours 7am-5pm; 🚌

Explore Ang Thong National Park above and below the sea with this tour company's kayaking and snorkelling day trips. Tour groups range from 30 to 45 people and the price includes the national park admission fee.

🏃 CANOPY ADVENTURES

☎ 0 7741 4150; www.canopyadventures thailand.com; booking office at Best Beach Bungalow, off Chaweng Beach Rd; adult/child 1700/1200B; ⌚ tours 10am, noon, 2pm & 3.30pm; 🚌

Be your own Tarzan on this zip-line course through the jungle. The 500m-long cable course is suspended 30m to 50m high between eight platforms. From your canopy eyrie, you can spy through the tree tops to the ocean.

🏃 DISCOVERY DIVERS

☎ 0 7741 3196; www.discoverydivers .com; Amari Palm Reef Resort, Chaweng Beach Rd; trips 4000-16,500B; ⌚ 10am-6pm

HOW TO PICK A DIVE COMPANY

Dive companies are held to high standards on Samui, where there's been an industry for nearly 20 years. So what distinguishes one from another? Price differences should signify a smaller class ratio and more emphasis on personal service than reputability or gear quality. Some dive shops on Samui transport customers via the commercial ferries to Ko Tao and from there they board the dive boat. This keeps costs down but it also expands the class size. For some, the more the merrier and the cheaper the better. But others might be willing to pay more for direct transport to the dive spots and fewer folks to share it with. Stop in at the shop to have a chat, meet the staff and ask about class sizes and costs. Also ask about the CoralWatch program (p92) if you've got an eco-streak.

A small and nimble operation, Discovery Divers limits trips to a maximum of 12 people and operates its own speedboat from Samui. The prices might be a little higher, but you get more attention and flexibility.

🎋 SAMUI INSTITUTE OF THAI CULINARY ARTS

☎ 0 7741 3172; www.sitca.net; Soi Colibri, Chaweng Beach Rd; classes 1850B; ⏱ 11am & 4pm; 🚌

Gain some curry courage at this Thai cooking school. Classes are held twice daily, last 2½ hours, and prepare from scratch a rotating menu of curries and side dishes.

🎋 SAMUI INTERNATIONAL DIVING SCHOOL

☎ 0 7742 2386; www.planet-scuba.net; Next to Soi Malibu Resort, Chaweng Beach Rd; dives 5000-15,000B; ⏱ 10am-10pm; 🚌

A veteran of the dive world, this full-service shop runs daily dive trips to the Samui archipelago's famous underwater sites. The most popular course is the open-water dive, a four-day beginner's course providing certification for dives up to 18m.

🛍 SHOP

There are plenty of opportunities to dispose of your baht. Chaweng Beach Rd is a 5km stretch filled with souvenir stalls and speciality stores.

🛍 CHANDRA BOUTIQUE
Clothing

☎ 08 6606 3639; www.chandra-exotic .com; 14/39 Chaweng Beach Rd; ⏱ 10am-midnight; 🚌

Ethno-chic has come a long way since those embroidered hemp sacks of yore. Chandra scours Asia, but mainly Bali, for wispy dresses that show off newly acquired suntans.

☐ DOODEE DÉCOR
Décor
☎ 08 1633 9160; Chaweng Beach Rd;
🕑 11am-11pm; 🚌

'Looks Good Decor' is the translation of this store's Thai name, which might make a third-grader giggle. Inside is a thoughtful collection of high-quality Thai-made gifts and home décor, like *dhana* vases, hand-hammered cutlery from Ayuthaya and funky embroidered handbags.

☐ MONKEY ISLAND
Clothing
☎ 0 7742 2778; Chaweng Beach Rd;
🕑 11am-10pm; 🚌

This glass-enclosed shop carries hip T-shirts emblazoned with Samui-inspired designs, like coconuts, tropical flowers and the island's name. But the designs are worldly enough to pass in nontouristy circles.

☐ PARAPHERNALIA
Décor
Chaweng Beach Rd; 🕑 11am-11pm; 🚌

Sharing space with Anton's Pasta Bar, this art shop sells décor pieces found in AKWA guesthouse, a few doors down. Perhaps your boudoir needs the cartoon-shaped Mr P lamps, with an anatomically

correct light switch, designed by the Bangkok-based Propaganda company.

☐ PHUKET MERMAIDS
Clothing
Chaweng Beach Rd; www.phuketmermaids.com; 🕑 11am-11pm; 🚌

If mermaids had a choice, they'd surely cast off their fish tails for these chic, sequined bikinis, made of high-quality lycra. One of 10 boutiques, this Thai-based company was founded by a Spanish businesswoman who wanted to solve the kingdom's shortage of undies and swimwear in foreigner sizes.

☐ SAAI BOOKSHOP
Bookshop
☎ 0 7741 3847; Chaweng Beach Rd;
🕑 10am-10pm; 🚌

Pick up some beach or plane reading at this friendly bookstore and travel agency.

COPY ARTISTS
From masterpieces to snapshots, the copy artists of Chaweng can turn any picture into an oil painting of striking resemblance. Always fancied a Rothko, love that Pacino sneer from *Scarface*? Or do you envision your own artistic medley? If you can sketch it or cut it out of a magazine, they can paint it and ship it home to you.

Browsing through the racks in search of a bargain at Vanities

VANITIES *Clothing*

Chaweng Beach Rd; ☼ **11am-10pm;** 🚌
Two fashion-studded gals from
Bangkok have opened this dress
boutique for the vacationing
urbanite. Selections hail from
Bangkok, Hong Kong and India,
and are a welcome relief from
the hippie chic of the beach's Bali
boutiques.

🍴 EAT

Like the ocean is to the thirsty,
Chaweng is to the hungry. The
beach road is filled with restaurants that charge First World prices
for local food served in pitiful
dieters' portions. Samui travellers
might be wealthier than years
past but they aren't morons. For
a memorable meal, sup on the
sand at the beachfront barbecues
or head inland toward Chaweng
Lake to find real Thai food being
bought and sold by local Thais.

🍴 AKWA RESTAURANT

Thai & International $$
☎ **08 4660 0551; AKWA Guesthouse,
28/12 Chaweng Beach Rd;** ☼ **8am-
midnight;** 🚌 ♿
Cartoon art takes a beach vaca-
tion at this youthful guesthouse
restaurant. Stop in for a jolt of
caffeine, all-day breakfasts or

a mango shake, and enjoy the restaurant's wall art that depicts famous cartoon characters in pop-art poses. The artwork was made by Chaweng's copy artists based on designs by the Australian owner.

🍴 BELLINI *Italian* $$$

☎ 0 7741 3831; 46/26 Soi Colibri, Chaweng Beach Rd; 🕙 noon-3pm & 6-11pm; 🚌

With the success of Vecchia Napoli, owner Francesco Vitagaliano has fashioned a more sophisticated restaurant among the upscale eateries on Soi Colibri. The menu is a gastronomic tour of Italy that is savoured in a crisp and romantic setting far from Chaweng's pizza and burger scene.

🍴 BETELNUT *Fusion* $$$

☎ 0 7741 3370; www.betelnutsamui .net; 43/4 Soi Colibri, Chaweng Beach Rd; 🕙 6-11pm

Fusion can be confusing, and often disappointing, but Betelnut will set you straight. Chef Jeffrey Lords claims an American upbringing and European culinary training, but most importantly he spent time in San Francisco, where all good food is born. The menu is a pan-Pacific mix of curries and chowder, papaya and pancetta.

🍴 CAFÉ AUX AMIS

Thai & French $$

☎ 0 7723 1169; Papillon Resort; Soi Baan Had Ngam, North Chaweng; 🕙 10am-10pm; 🚼

Usually a high-powered view like this – stretching from Ko Matlang to the tip of Chaweng Noi – should cost a lot more, but Café Aux Amis is friendly to small spenders. The open-air restaurant is casual chic with a menu that expertly, but unpretentiously, fuses French and Thai cuisine. Enjoy the *poisson avec trois sauces* (basically Thai-style

---

SOI COLIBRI

The past 10 years have brought remarkable change to Chaweng. Coconut trees have been replaced first by budget bungalows and now by multistorey resorts. It won't be long before the beach road will morph from a low-slung mishmash of shacks to urban-style outdoor malls. If we could be so bold as to request a future look for Chaweng, let Soi Colibri serve as a blueprint. This short lane is located at the southern end of the beach across from Centara Grand Beach Resort Samui. The restored Chinese-style shophouses contain gastronomically accomplished restaurants, like pan-Pacific Betelnut (see above) and contemporary Italian Bellini (see above), and are a welcome relief from central Chaweng's hyperactivity. If another 10 years is a mellowing agent for Chaweng, perhaps we'll long for the lost days of neon and techno, in a perennial mourning for youth.

Dining on the rooftop at Captain Kirk

grilled fish with a French accent) and creamy *gratin dauphinois*.

🍴 CAPTAIN KIRK
International $$
☎ 08 1270 5376; Chaweng Beach Rd;
⏰ 11am-10pm; 🚌 🚲
When the crew is hungry and cranky, make your escape to this rooftop garden restaurant for views of Chaweng Lake and the busy beach road. Mixed seafood grills, served with French fries, is a crowd pleaser and so is the final bill.

🍴 E-SAN YAM SABB *Thai* $
Chaweng Beach Rd; ⏰ 4-10pm; 🚌 🚲
If you're commitment-shy when

it comes to eating in a restaurant, sate your hunger at this eat-and-dash stall that fixes an assortment of Thai wok dishes, from *râht nâh* (stir-fried noodles with gravy) to fried rice. With this cheap and tasty food as ballast, you're ready to allocate your caloric intake to a river of cold beer.

🍴 GRINGO'S CANTINA
Tex-Mex $$
☎ 08 1892 1416; www.gringoscantina samui.com; 166/79 Moo 2; ⏰ dinner
Wash down a Tex-Mex classic with a jug of sangria or a frozen margarita. We liked the chimichangas (mostly because we like saying chimichanga). There are burgers, pizzas and vegie options too, if

you don't feel like going 'south of the border'.

🍴 LAEM DIN MARKET & NIGHT MARKET
Thai $

Soi 3, Chaweng Beach Rd; 🕐 **market 4am-6pm, night market 6pm-2am;** 👶
A busy day market, Laem Din is packed with stalls selling fresh fruits, vegetables and meats that stock local Thai kitchens. Pick up a kilo of sweet green oranges or wander the stalls trying to spot the ingredients in last night's curry. For dinner, come to the adjacent night market and sample tasty southern-style fried chicken and curries.

🍴 PAGE RESTAURANT
Thai & International $$-$$$
☎ 07742 2767; www.thelibrary.name; **Library Resort, Chaweng Beach Rd;** 🕐 **noon-11pm;** 🚇
Almost institutional in its mini-malism, the Page is a pleasant excuse to explore Samui's latest

fashion plate, the Library Resort. Ultra-austere, the Library's pod-like buildings face each other across a trim lawn alleviating the claustrophobia of Chaweng. The window-ensconced restaurant faces the sea and focuses on simplicity: a menu the size of an index card and a view of infinite beauty.

🍴 PEE SOON *Thai* $$
☎ 08 1271 4636; **Chaweng Food Center, Soi 4, btwn Chaweng Lake & Chaweng Beach Rd;** 🕐 **5pm-2am;** 👶
Far from pretty but decidedly delicious, Pee Soon specialises in seafood barbecues for Samui residents. The ice tray in front shows off the day's catch and the cacophonous kitchen at the back fills the tables with a delicate balance of sweet, spicy and sour side dishes, such as green curry, garlic-pepper squid and the house speciality, clams stir-fried with chilli paste.

NICE EYES: PICKING FRESH FISH
At night, the beaches are lit up with fairy lights for the evening ritual of beach barbecues. Tables are planted in the sand and ice trays of fresh fish display the dinner options. Now all you have to do is pick the freshest, most delicious fish and enjoy the scenery. Common wisdom says that the unclouded eyes of a fish are a sign of freshness, but picking a tasty fish variety always seems to be a more daunting task. King prawns are the most exotic options for foreigners but butterfish (also known as white pomfret) is one of the Thais' favourites. Whether steamed or grilled, the flesh cleaves away from the bone easily so that most cooks prepare the fish whole. The tastiest meat is just under the cheeks.

🍴 PREGO *Italian* $$$
☎ 0 7742 2015; Amari Palm Reef Resort, Chaweng Beach Rd; 🕐 6-11pm
Prego has discarded the trattoria uniform of chequered table-cloths in favour of a barely-there dining room consisting of cool marble and modern geometry. The crowds adore the plate-sized pieces of art, from spinach-stuffed raviolis to a minisculpture of ti-ramisu. Reservations are accepted for two seatings a night, at 7pm and 9pm.

🍴 SOJENG KITCHEN *Thai* $
☎ 08 1892 2841; 155/9 Chaweng Beach Rd; 🕐 11-2am; 🚌 ⛓
Picking a good Thai restaurant is a lot like that old Motown tune about picking a pretty girl to be your wife. If you want to be happy for the rest of your life, or at least for dinner, don't pick a pretty restaurant. Instead opt for a plain Jane, who can, like Sojeng, whip up a wonderful meal with a few clangs of the spatula against the wok.

🍴 VECCHIA NAPOLI
Italian $$-$$$
☎ 08 7277 6493; Soi Solo, Chaweng Beach Rd; 🕐 11am-11pm; 🚌 ⛓
Thin-crust pizzas are delivered out of a traditional Neapolitan wood-fired oven as if they were gifts from the gods. And these celestial creations strike that perfect pizza balance – garlicky, gooey and creamy.

🍴 WAVE SAMUI
Thai & International $$
☎ 0 7723 0803; 11/5 Chaweng Beach Rd; 🕐 8-1.30am; ⛓
Everyone says that Samui is going upscale, but the most crowded res-taurants at dinnertime are still the old-fashioned budget spots, like Wave Samui. This jack-of-all trades (guesthouse-bar-restaurant) serves honest food at honest prices and fosters a travellers ambience with an in-house library and a popular happy hour (3pm to 7pm).

🍴 ZICO'S *Brazilian* $$$
☎ 0 7723 1560-3; www.zicossamui.com; 🕐 5pm-1am
This palatial churrascaria puts the carne in Carnival. Vegetar-ians should beware – Zico's is an all-you-can-eat Brazilian meat-fest, and it comes complete with saucy dancers sporting peacock-like outfits.

DRINK
The whole island comes to Chaweng to party and nightfall powers up a rowdy assortment of neon, techno and whisky buckets. The party goes until 2am at least, sometimes later if no-one is

Unwinding outdoors at Ark Bar

looking. Most bars and clubs are situated in two U-shaped sois: Soi Green Mango and Soi Solo (also known as 'Soi Starbucks').

♈ ARK BAR *Bar*
☎ 0 7742 2047; www.ark-bar.com; Garden Beach Resort, Hat Chaweng; 🕙 4pm-2am

It isn't a secret: Chaweng's best feature is its beach, perhaps most spectacular as the day's hubbub settles into inky night. The beach-front Ark Bar specialises in laid-back tropical clichés: paper lanterns bobbing in the evening breeze, Thai axe pillows for lounging and an international clientele of young backpackers and mature travellers savouring the holiday glow.

♈ BAR SOLO *Bar*
☎ 0 7741 4012; Soi Solo, Chaweng Beach Rd; 🕙 2pm-2am

A sign of things to come, Bar Solo has future-fitted Chaweng's outdoor beer halls into an urban setting with sleek cubist décor and a cocktail list that doesn't scream holiday hayseed. The evening drink specials lure in the front-loaders preparing for a late, late night at the dance clubs on Soi Solo and Soi Green Mango.

♈ BLACK JACK PUB *Bar*
☎ 0 7741 3214; Soi Green Mango, Chaweng Beach Rd; 🕙 5-11pm

A home away from home, this English-style pub has soothed the occasional tropical malaise for

SHITFACE BUCKETS

Like getting drunk but hate wasting time drinking? Thailand has invented the mother-of-all booze bombs: the Red Bull bucket, which contains Coke, Red Bull energy drink (a product of Thailand) and a pint of vodka or local Thai whisky. The concoction is mixed unceremoniously in a bucket with ice and festooned with straws so that booze hounds can share in the attack. The mixture goes down easy, real easy, and catapults drinkers from slightly tipsy to totally shitfaced in half the time of beer. Wednesday beach parties at Ark Bar (see p49) and other beachfront bars serve buckets by the, well, bucket loads, along with house music and the pounding surf.

12 years. But its main draw card is EuroSport Live complete with commentary. Free internet, same-day newspapers, toasties and lots of penny-pinching drink specials make Jack a reliable bar-hopping mate.

▼ EASY TIME BAR *Bar*
Chaweng Beach Rd; 🕙 **8pm-2am**
Too old for techno, too young for bed? Then you might be an eternal flower child in need of a dive bar. This closet-sized spot obliges with graffiti on the wall, dreadlocked bartenders and requisite Bob Marley tunes. Globetrotting regulars describe it as a 'grassroots' reggae bar and a good conversation starter is an inquiry into your stool mates' travel itinerary.

▼ GOOD KARMA *Bar*
☎ **0 7741 3857; Chaweng Beach Rd;** 🕙 **8.30am-late**
Open all day, this snazzy lounge lures the hip 'hi-so' (Thai high soci-ety) crowd with canopied daybeds and a hidden pond.

▼ NATHALIE'S ART PALACE
Bar
☎ **0 7723 1485; www.nathalies-life style.com; 486 Soi 4, near Chaweng Lake;** 🕙 **7-11.30pm**
You've got to hand it to German TV personality Nathalie Gutermann for her unabashed self-promotion. She's turned a hillside apartment into a boutique hotel and bar, which primarily promote the cult of Nathalie and her 'fabulous' lifestyle. Curious about the life of an expatriate claiming aristocratic origins? Stop by for a sunset cocktail, Friday night barbecue or some of the special party events.

▼ TROPICAL MURPHY'S *Bar*
☎ **0 7741 3614; 14/40 Chaweng Beach Rd;** 🕙 **noon-2am**
Like banana pancakes and mango lassis, Irish bars have flourished in the unlikeliest corners of the

traveller trail with a winning formula of suds and sociability. With all the trappings of a pub outfitted with sandals and beachwear, Tropical Murphy's fills that all-important cocktail hour, just after sunbathing and before dinner. Catch it any later and the convivial crowd will be off foraging for food.

 PLAY

Once you've got your beer swerve on, Chaweng also has a handful of dance clubs playing vacation Top 40, house beats or reggae standards.

⭐ CLUB SOLO *Club*

☎ 08 9724 6334; Soi Solo, Chaweng Beach Rd; ⏲ 2-6am

Don't worry party princess, you don't have to go to bed once Green Mango closes. This after-party venue is ready to come to

the rescue with more music and mayhem to fill the pre-dawn hours.

⭐ COCO BLUES *Live Music*

☎ 0 7741 4354; Chaweng Beach Rd; ⏲ 6pm-2am

At the north end of Chaweng, Coco Blues reinterprets New Orleans-style hedonism for Samui. The multi-storey bar and restaurant is best known for its live music (every night, except Tuesday, at 9pm) ranging from jazz to blues to cover tunes. For visual entertainment, check out the street-side bar overlooking Chaweng's manic traffic.

⭐ GREEN MANGO *Club*

☎ 0 7742 2661; www.greenmango group.com; Soi Green Mango, Chaweng Beach Rd; ⏲ 8pm-3am

One of Samui's original discos, Green Mango is where all of the late-night zombies head after

PARTY MOON

In this Buddhist land, most religious holidays are pegged to the lunar calendar. Either a cultural nod or a sacrilegious phenomenon, the parties that dominate the island's nightlife follow suit, honouring the waxing and waning of the night sky's silver body. It all started with Ko Pha-Ngan's Full Moon party (see p98) and has been copy-catted on Samui with a Black Moon party (held once a month on the new moon) and an Escape Party (held twice a month in between the two moons). Samui's lunar parties are held at Chaweng Lake View, an open-air stage on the west side of Chaweng Lake, and usually get started after midnight. The island's resident DJs and occasionally a superstar spinner, grace the stage. Q Bar (see p52) and other Chaweng clubs sponsor after-parties so that the moon doesn't go to bed alone. Parties are well advertised across the island, so don't worry about watching the night sky.

downing their drinks elsewhere. There aren't a lot of bells and whistles in this open-air warehouse – just late-night music, dancing and drinking with enough sweating bodies to make it a true party.

⭐ MINT BAR *Club*
☎ 08 7089 8726; Soi Solo, Chaweng Beach Rd; 🕙 10pm-2am

The street scene on this party street is too entertaining to keep the crowds corralled in this stylish club on ordinary nights. But the Mint is able to lure a few DJ heavyweights for a Samui spin on extraordinary nights. Watch the entertainment listings for special events.

⭐ Q BAR SAMUI *Club*
☎ 0 7741 3297; www.qbarsamui.com; Khao Hua Jook, above Chaweng Lake; 🕙 6pm-2am

Overlooking Chaweng Lake, Q Bar is a little piece of Bangkok nightlife planted among the coconut trees. The upstairs lounge opens just before sunset treating cocktail connoisseurs to various highbrow tipples and a drinkable view of southern Chaweng – mountains, sea and sky. After 10pm, the night-crawlers descend upon the downstairs club where DJs spin the crowd into a techno amoeba. A taxi there will cost between 200B and 300B.

Enjoying the lake view at Q Bar Samui

BEACHES & TOWNS

CHAWENG

GAY SAMUI

Samui doesn't have the high-profile gay scene that you'll find in Bangkok or Phuket, but you can tap into the community at the **Three Gems Project** (☎ 0 7743 1837; opposite Centara Grand Beach Samui Resort, Chaweng Beach Rd). In this restored shophouse, you'll find three gay-run, gay-friendly businesses: Emerald Green Spa, Ruby Red Lounge and Sapphire Blue Restaurant. For more gay-friendly listings visit **Thai Boy** (www.thaiboy.net/guide), **Dreaded Ned** (www.dreadedned.com) and **Utopia** (www.utopia-asia.com).

⭐ **REGGAE PUB** *Bar/Club*
☎ 0 7742 2331; Soi Reggae, near Chaweng Lake; 🕒 9pm-2am
It isn't a beach holiday if you haven't heard Bob Marley, never mind that Thailand is a long way from Jamaica. The Land of Smiles loves the Rasta prophet and this long-running venue is something of a Samui institution, though it is best loved by Samui veterans. After the clock strikes midnight, the soundtrack switches to house music and younger techno-heads occasionally migrate here from Soi Green Mango. A taxi there will set you back between 200B and 300B.

>LAMAI

It is hard to be the runner-up beach behind flamboyant Chaweng. Just as pretty and blonde, Lamai has a bit of an identity complex. It is the birthplace of Samui's fasting culture thanks to Spa Samui's two Lamai branches. Visitors hoping to clean up their lives and their spirits arrive here with visions of an earthly nirvana. Instead they find lascivious Lamai, where the commercial strip is a tad tatty with boozy bar girls being the primary local ambassadors. The international visitors of Lamai tend to hail from the working-class ranks of Western countries, sporting an affinity for tattoos and motorcycle clubs. Health nuts and hedonists seem unlikely companions until you consider that even in the smallest towns, churches and bars tend to congregate together.

The southern end of the beach has a more old-fashioned, castaway feel that used to be Samui's trademark. The family-run guesthouses are built along sandy roads in between chicken coops and yawning dogs.

LAMAI

⊙ SEE
Hin-Ta Hin-Yai 1 A4

🏃 DO
Spa Samui Beach............2 D1

🏠 SHOP
Health Mart..................3 A1
Hin Ta Hin Yai Market.....4 A4

🍴 EAT
Coast Restaurant............5 B2
Go Wat.......................6 C1
Kokomiko 7 A3
Lamai Day Market 8 C1
Lamai Night Food Centre..9 B2
Radiance Restaurant....(see 2)
Sabeinglae 10 A4
Srinuan Thai Food
   Restaurant 2..............11 B3
Will Wait.....................12 B2

🍸 DRINK
Bauhaus......................13 B2
Beach Republic............14 E1
Samui Shamrock 15 B2
Shark Bar & Buddy
   Beer.........................16 D1

SEE

HIN TA HIN YAI

Off Ring Rd (Rd 4169), South Lamai; admission free; ⏰ 6am-6pm; 🚌
Lamai beach is weighted by massive boulders but none are as spectacular as the grandparent rocks, an honorific name considering that Grandfather Rock looks like an erect penis and Grandmother looks like the female counterpart. Don't be shy about posing with Grandpa, even the monks take the photo-op. On a serious note, assigning human characteristics to rock formations is a common feature in Southeast Asian Muslim culture.

DO

SPA SAMUI BEACH

☎ 0 7723 0855; www.spasamui.com; Ring Rd, North Lamai; massages 300-650B; ⏰ 10am-6pm; 🚌

SWIMMING WARNINGS
Chaweng and Lamai can have strong surf and riptides, especially during the rainy season. The hotels will usually post warnings of swimming hazards and conditions on a beach board or warning flags. If you are caught in a riptide, which is a strong surface current heading seaward, it is advised not to fight it, but instead to swim parallel to the shore to exit the current or float along with it until it dissipates in deeper water.

The original branch of the renowned Spa Samui Resorts, which established Thailand as a destination for cleansing and fasting tourism, Spa Samui Beach (better known as Spa Beach) is located in a busy, but convenient, corner of Lamai. On-site spa treatments and wellness classes are open to day-use visitors. Come for a post-beach massage, healing clay facial or a wholesome meal at

Rock formations at Hin Ta Hin Yai

Radiance Restaurant (see p61). For more information on their fasting program, see p16. A complimentary shuttle travels between this branch and Spa Samui Village.

✈ SPA SAMUI VILLAGE
☎ 0 7723 0976; www.spasamui.com; North Lamai; massages 300-650B; ⏱ 10am-6pm

The second Spa Samui branch, Spa Samui Village (or Spa Village) camps out on the side of a forested mountain. Steep paths lead from reception to the yoga and massage *salas* (open pavilions) overlooking the bushy headdresses of the coconut trees. The setting is rustic and peaceful, perfect for steeping in the herbal steam cave or breathing deeply during a yoga session. For more information on their fasting program, see p16.

YOGA IN THE TREES
Let your yoga practice out of those sweaty closets at one of Samui's many open-air pavilions (known as *sala* in Thai). Perched in the trees, you might begin to enjoy the mandatory *shavasana*, or finally find that belly-originating breath. Spa Samui Village (see above) holds morning meditation and Iyengar classes in a hillside *sala* in Lamai. Kamalaya Koh Samui (p69) has a breathtaking view of the ocean from its cliff-side *sala* as well as a full menu of yoga varieties, from Ashtanga to Hatha.

A complimentary shuttle travels between this branch and Spa Samui Beach.

✈ TAMARIND SPRINGS
☎ 0 7723 0571; www.tamarindsprings.com; 205/7 Moo 4, Maret, North Lamai; spa treatments 2600-8500B; ⏱ 10am-8pm

More like a spa journey than a day spa, Tamarind Springs incorporates an exploration of the natural world into its steam baths and spa treatments. Follow the path to the steam room carved into towering boulders, plunge into the pool dappled in sunlight and then pad softly to the massage pavilion serenaded by bird song. For more information on Tamarind Springs, see p19.

🛍 SHOP
🛍 HEALTH MART *Beauty*
☎ 0 7741 9157; 104/1 Ring Rd; ⏱ 8am-5pm; 🚌 ♿

Considering the number of people wandering around Lamai on fasts, there are very few wellness stores. Affiliated with Spa Samui, Health Mart, only 100m from Wat Lamai, carries several natural body and beauty lines produced by royally sponsored economic development projects. Look for the herbal shower gels and shampoos made by Khao Kho Talay Pu, Supaporn facial scrubs, Tropicana coconut shampoos and Power of Brown tea.

WHY IS THE OCEAN BLUE?

Samui's turquoise waters are merely an optical illusion, in some respects. Try holding the jewel-toned water in your hands and the water is clear and colourless. But from the beach, you enjoy the visual splendour of light's colour spectrum being absorbed and scattered. Water molecules easily absorb red, yellow and green wavelengths of light, leaving the blue and violet waves visible to the human eye. Shallow water tends to reflect more blue and some green light than deep water, which reflects only a small amount of blue, making it appear blue-black. Organisms and suspended materials in the water also affect light reflection and absorption. The ocean also has a mirror-like quality reflecting the changing hues of the sky above.

📷 HIN TA HIN YAI MARKET
Souvenirs

Off Ring Rd, South Lamai; ⏱ **8am-6pm;**
🚌 ♿

Along the road leading to the Grandfather and Grandmother Rocks are small souvenir shops catering to the sightseeing impulse shopper. There is however a cultural angle here: the pyramid shaped candies are *kà·lá·mair,* a local caramel made with either coconut (the brown ones) or pandanus (the green ones).

🍴 EAT

Lamai has some real gems in the restaurant category but they tend to be far-flung. In central Lamai, the options are the usual expat grub shops that dominate every tourist area in Thailand. You are on your own if you get a hankering for a meat pie.

🍴 CLIFF BAR & GRILL
Mediterranean $$$

☎ 0 7741 4266; www.thecliffsamui
.com; Ring Rd, btwn Lamai & Chaweng;
⏱ kitchen noon-10pm, bar noon-2am;
🚌

With the mother of all views, the Cliff teeters on an oceanfront ridge caressed by a jungle-fringed headland that frames the interplay of sea and sky. The outdoor tables enjoy colourful dishes of Mediterranean cuisine, whose zesty flavours balance the humidity outside while soothing homesick tastebuds.

🍴 COAST RESTAURANT
Thai & International $$$

☎ 0 7742 4550; www.lamaiwanta.com;
Lamai Wanta Resort, Lamai Beach Rd;
⏱ 10am-9pm; 🚌 ♿

It is easy to please people when they're on vacation, but Coast tries a little harder than most. The beachfront restaurant delivers a

Night-time views at Cliff Bar & Grill

main course of scenery as well as considerate international and Thai dishes.

🍴 GO WAT *Thai* $

Off Ring Rd, next to Lamai Fresh Market; 🕐 5.30pm-2am; 🚻

This greasy-spoon restaurant does cheap and tasty Thai food and is best known for its *grà·dòok mŏo tôrt* (pork ribs). Although its hours are erratic, when the doors are open, the fans march in obediently.

🍴 KOKOMIKO
International $$

☎ 0 7742 4289; Ring Rd, South Lamai; 🕐 6-10pm; 🚌 🚻

Don't let the ringside location beside the Ring Rd scare you off. Kokomiko is a lot like dinner at a friend's house, if the friend is a professional cook. This is better-than home cooking with homey hospitality. Try the pepper steak, which is toothy Thai beef bathed in a signature coconut milk and peppercorn sauce. Come before 7pm to get a seat.

🍴 LAMAI DAY MARKET
Thai $

Off Ring Rd; 🕐 6am-8pm; 🚌 🚻 ♿

This is a hive of activity, selling food necessities and takeaway. Visit the covered area to pick up fresh fruit or to see vendors shred-

Tossing the wok at Lamai Night Food Centre

ding coconuts to make coconut milk. Or find the ice cream seller for homemade coconut ice cream. It's next door to a petrol station.

🍴 LAMAI NIGHT FOOD CENTRE *Thai* $

Lamai Beach Rd; 🕑 **6-2am;** ♿ ♿
Eating becomes a circus sideshow at Lamai's outdoor food centre, next door to a 7-Eleven. The vendor stalls whip up all the Thai standards – a spectacle in itself. And then the hostesses at the nearby girly bars crank up the music for pole dancing or a few rounds of *muay thai* (Thai boxing). All in all an absurd underbelly stew.

🍴 RADIANCE RESTAURANT *Thai & Vegetarian* $$

North Lamai; 🕑 **6.30am-9.30pm;** ♿ Ⓥ
Fill your belly with a healthy meal at one of Spa Samui's restaurants. The menu includes vegetarian and vegan meals that are friendly to post-fasters. The restaurant at Spa Samui Beach (p57) sits on a pretty stretch of beach, but the one at Spa Samui Village (p57) is perfectly perched to watch a forest wake up. A complimentary shuttle travels between the two.

🍴 ROCKY'S *International* $$$

☎ **0 7723 3020; www.rockyresort.com; 438/1 Moo 1;** 🕑 **lunch & dinner**

Easily the top dining spot on Lamai, Rocky's gourmet dishes are actually a bargain when you convert the baht into your native currency. Try the signature beef tenderloin with blue cheese. On Tuesday evenings, diners enjoy a special Thai-themed evening with a prepared menu of local delicacies. Rocky's is located at the like-named resort just south of Lamai.

🍴 SABEINGLAE *Thai* $$

☎ **08 1538 7045; 438/82 Ring Rd;** 🕑 **6pm-midnight;** ♿
'Everything there is delicious,' said our cab driver as he dropped us off. And indeed this rustic seafood shack, known for its Samui cuisine,

---

WEATHER THREE WAYS

Samui has roughly three seasons: dry, hot and wet. Starting at the peak of the tourist season (December to February), the weather is dry with northeast winds that stir up high waves along the exposed west coast. The wind dies down from March to July when air temperatures climb up to 40°C. The seas get quieter and the tides lower during this time. From July to September, the island starts to get a few refreshing afternoon showers. The serious daily soakers don't start until October and November and are accompanied by rough seas. In general Samui gets less rain than the Andaman coast.

delivered a table full of intensely delicious creations, like *wai kôo·a* (a coconut milk curry with octopus), *yam tá·lair sà·mǔi* (a zesty local-style salad) and a seaweed dish whose name has been forgotten. The Samui dishes appear in the menu in Thai only, so ask your server for recommendations. It's south of Hin Ta Hin Yai.

🍴 SRINUAN THAI FOOD RESTAURANT 2 *Thai* $-$$
124/357 Lamai Beach Rd; 🕑 **6-10pm;** 👶 ♿

If you judge your food by its restaurant packaging, then you'll overlook such simple wok shops as Srinuan. With only a collection of plastic tables and chairs, Srinuan has expanded its bare-bones operation from the Lamai Night Food Centre to this second location, where it grills and stir-fries fish, clams and prawns like a celebrity chef.

🍴 WILL WAIT
Thai & International $$
☎ **0 7742 4263; Lamai Beach Rd;** 🕑 **11am-11pm;** 🚌 👶 Ⓥ

Breakfast and lunch are always a hit at this reliable standard. Introduce yourself to the Thai version of an American breakfast: runny eggs, white toast and lightweight coffee. Or get to know the Thai basics with their English-friendly menu. There is another branch in Chaweng.

🍸 DRINK

When it comes to nightlife, Lamai sits on the other side of the 'tracks' from Chaweng. Lamai attracts a true grit, working-class crowd to its open-air bars. The clientele are veteran bar-stool stoopers, who seem naked without a cigarette and drink in hand. Girly bars take centre stage here too, whereas in Chaweng they get relegated to a few back streets. A smaller minority are the fasters who are rewarding their good behaviour with a pint or two or three…

🍸 BAUHAUS CLUB
Club
☎ **0 7741 8387; Lamai Beach Rd;** 🕑 **2pm-2am**

A long-running club, Bauhaus does a little bit of everything – from chill-out beer swilling to wannabe Ibiza dance parties. Despite its central Lamai location, it is uncommonly unseedy, dare we say, wholesome. On a recent visit, the twice-weekly foam parties were a hit with the under-12 set.

🍸 BEACH REPUBLIC *Lounge*
www.beachrepublic.com; 176/34 Moo 4

Recognised by its yawning thatch-patched awnings, Beach Republic would be the perfect spot to shoot one of those MTV Spring Break episodes. There's an inviting wading pool, comfy lounge chairs and an endless cocktail list.

⛾ SAMUI SHAMROCK *Bar*
☎ 08 1597 8572; www.samui-shamrock.com; 124/144 Lamai Beach Rd; ⏲ 9-2am

More classic than chic, Samui Shamrock is a good-times pub where house bands belt out cover tunes that inspire the tipsy crowd to sing along. At some point in the night you'll hear 'Hotel California', the ultimate foreigner tribute song.

⛾ SHARK BAR & BUDDY BEER *Bar*
☎ 0 7745 8080; 173/24 Ring Rd, North Lamai; ⏲ noon-2am

With a nose for money, Bangkok's Buddy group has transplanted its gentrifying business model to the downmarket shores of Lamai beach. The company successfully upgraded Bangkok's Khao San Rd and will probably do the same with its new Lamai venture, including a boutique hotel, restaurant (misnomered Buddy Beer) and the techno-thumping Shark Bar.

>SOUTH COAST & INLAND

Heading south from Lamai, the Ring Rd (Rd 4169) makes a hard turn at Hua Thanon and the frenetic pace begins to downshift. This is the most traditional part of the island with glimpses of Samui's past as 'coconut island'. Sleepy little lives unfold under the shade trees, chickens scratch after grubs, and water buffalo slowly chew through the day.

The southeastern corner has the greatest concentration of nonbeach attractions: the fishing village of Hua Thanon, Samui Butterfly Garden and the inland waterfalls. Pinned between the two headlands, the coastline of Bang Kao is wild and windswept, better for meditative strolls than sunbathing and swimming.

Further west is Thong Krut, a fishing village lined with weather-worn seaside restaurants and used as a jumping-off point for day trips to Ko Taen and Ko Matsom. You can explore this coast with a plan, or you can weave your way through village and grove along winding Rd 4170, allowing whimsy to be your guide.

SOUTH COAST & INLAND

BEACHES & TOWNS

SOUTH COAST & INLAND

◉ SEE
◉ BAN HUA THANON

Ring Rd; 🚌 ♿

Welcome to a morsel of southern Thailand, with a sprinkling of Muslim Thais living beside Buddhist Thais. The old wooden houses, only 50 to 60 years old, have weathered beyond their years, looking more ancient than antique. Pick your way through the parked motorcycles to the pier where the fisherfolk moor their small but stately boats. Continue to Hua Thanon Market (see p71) and further on to the local mosque and the village's Muslim quarter.

◉ BUDDHA FOOTPRINT

Wat Phra Raow Taow, Rd 4170, Ban Harn;
🕙 **8am-6pm**

More religious than touristy, the Buddha Footprint is housed in a hill-side chapel. The room-sized sculpture of the sole of Buddha's foot is believed to be about 100 years old – nearly prehistoric for Samui – and is a common symbolic representation of the enlightened one. The temple's abbot asks that people show respect by being quiet and not eating and drinking at the site.

◉ CHEDI LAEM SAW

Rd 4170, Laem Saw, Ban Kao; ♿

A wild and rocky stretch of beach is barely tamed by this lonely stupa

Soak in the atmosphere at Ban Hua Thanon

TEMPLE ETIQUETTE

Samui's temples aren't as stunning or as formal as the royally associated temples of Bangkok. But despite their humble façade, it is important to observe certain rules of conduct.

> Take off your shoes, hat and sunglasses before entering a building.
> Leave a small donation (20B).
> *Wâi* (perform the Thai greeting to) the central Buddha.
> Stand to the back or side of the chapel so that worshippers have access to the altar.

staked into a spit of land. Nearby is a meditation forest and another hilltop stupa. Follow the signs for 'Waikiki Bungalows' to reach the *chedi* from the main road.

◉ MAGIC GARDEN
🕑 9am-6pm

A fruit farmer laboured in the jungle in the Samui interior to create this spiritual garden of concrete characters depicting Buddhist myths and legends. The road here is a military road north of Ban Saket, and a little tough for most vehicles, so visitors are advised to take one of the jungle tours available through the travel agents.

◉ MEDITATION CAVE
Kamalaya Koh Samui, Laem Set Rd, Laem Set; visitors pass 600B

Make a spa date with Kamalaya (p69) so you can sneak a peek at this decades old cave temple built by local monks for meditation. Temple caves are a vital part of the forest temple tradition in Thailand and in the past, monks have lived inside the cave as meditation hermits. The visitors pass allows access to the cave as well as use of the health resort's steam cavern and plunge pools.

◉ NAM TOK NA MUANG 1
Off Ring Rd, Ban Thurian; admission free

One of two nearby waterfalls, this 18m-high cascade is an easy walk from the car park and is the best example of Thais' peculiar appreciation of falling water: a quick snapshot, a bowl of noodles, a few souvenirs and back in the car. For lolly-gaggers, Na Muang also has elephant trekking (see Waterfall Jungle Treks, p69) and is a popular stop on the package-tour route.

◉ NAM TOK NA MUANG 2
Off Ring Rd, Ban Thurian; admission 250B

The taller of the sister waterfalls, this one crashes 80m and sifts out the spectators from the enthusiasts with an admission fee and a 30-minute walk. The falls are more dramatic and there's a natural swimming pool at the base but it is still a stop on the package-tour route. Next to the entrance is a

BEACHES & TOWNS

SOUTH COAST & INLAND

MINDING MATTER

The southern coast is windy and lonely, and once a favourite meditation area for monks who found spiritual inspiration along this rocky stretch, burying shrines in the cave crevices – a tradition of forest temples adapted for the sea. Today, Kamalaya (opposite) and Yoga Thailand (opposite), two health retreats, have modernised mindfulness on the coast.

zip-line, known locally as 'skyfox', and elephant treks.

NAM TOK WANG SAOTONG

Off Ring Rd, Ban Tha Po; admission free
With a 1km walk from the car park, this waterfall is less crowded than Na Muang and more of a communion with nature than with your fellow sightseers. To get here, turn right off the Ring Rd at Wat Khunaram and follow the road past Baan Chang Elephant Trekking.

SAMUI BUTTERFLY GARDEN

☎ 0 7742 4020; Laem Set Rd, Laem Set; adult/child 170/100B; ⏱ 8.30am-5.30pm
Walk slowly among the tropical flowers to spot the colourful butterflies fanning their wings as they sip nectar. At first only a few will cross your path, but search the garden for the sultriest flowers to find an undulating carpet of anxious diners. Butterflies are most active in the mornings. It's opposite Central Samui Village.

WAT KHUNARAM

Ring Rd, btwn Ban Thurian & Ban Hua Thanon; donations accepted; ⏱ 9am-6pm; 🚌
Some temples are famous for their architecture or sculptures, but this pilgrimage site is a fixture in the abbot adoration tradition. Luang Phaw Daeng (Phra Kru Samathak-ittikhon) was a master meditator in the 1940s and 1950s, and his preserved corpse, complete with sunglasses, remains on display as inspiration.

Mummified monk at Wat Khunaram

BEACHES & TOWNS

SOUTH COAST & INLAND

☺ WAT SAMRET
☎ 0 7723 3051; off Ring Rd, btwn Ban Thurian & Ban Hua Thanon; ⏰ 9am-6pm; 🚌
Temple buffs will find a dusty gem in Wat Samret, which has a white marble Buddha, believed to have come from Burma or India, and a crowded hall of expressionless Buddha figures. Across the Ring Rd is the Coral Buddha, used as a shrine by the Wat Samret monks. Ask for directions at the temple.

🏃 DO

🏃 KAMALAYA KOH SAMUI
☎ 0 7742 9800; www.kamalaya.com; Laem Set Rd, Laem Set; spa packages 6400B
With a breathtaking setting, this wellness resort breathes new life into burnt-out professionals. Billed as a holistic spa, it offers a little of everything: yoga, detox, Chinese medicine, spa treatments and weight-loss programs. Open-air salas (pavilions) pose dutifully upon a sapphire ocean and forested pathways respectfully bypass ancient boulders. The spa and classes are open to nonguests with advance reservations.

🏃 WATERFALL JUNGLE TREKS
Nam Tok Na Muang 1 & 2, Ban Thurian; treks 600-1200B; ⏰ 9am-5pm

At each of the two waterfalls is an elephant camp that gives tourists the bragging rights of balancing on the backs of patient pachyderms. Tours trudge through the jungle for 30 minutes or an hour.

🏃 YOGA THAILAND
☎ 0 7744 7245; www.yoga-thailand .com; Ban Kao; 7-day programs 28,600B
Serious yoga students come to this centre to further their Ashtanga practice. Paul and Jutima, a husband-and-wife team, run the centre, one of the few certified by Sri K Pattabhi Jois. Paul's chief teacher was OP Tiwari, Pranayama master and classical yogi. They conduct residential retreats and host renowned yoga teachers.

ISLAND HOPPING
Skip across the waves on a long-tail fishing boat to Ko Taen and Ko Matsom, two barely populated islands offshore from Thong Krut. Ko Taen has some snorkelling, a small Muslim fishing village and a guesthouse. Ko Matsom is an uninhabited island with a few sunbathing spots. Everyone in Thong Krut with a mobile phone can arrange a day trip to these islands, but most folks stop at one of the seaside restaurants or guesthouses to make arrangements. Trips usually last four to five hours and cost 1500B for the boat (seating up to five people).

Somporn Somwang,
Jack-of-all-trades and host of 'Old Stories' radio show on 94.5 Samui Radio

What do you do for a living? I used to work for the government in Bangkok with an agricultural technology program. Now I'm a jungle person. I live here in the jungle with my garden. **What did you miss most about Samui?** I missed my family. The value of Thai culture is being grateful to your parents. They need you when they are old and sick. I returned to Samui to take care of my mother after my father died. **How had the island changed?** I came back and everyone was getting rich. But I'm willing to be poor in order to be true to myself. **What advice do you have for the future of Samui?** I can't stop development but people should listen to the king and respect land, earth, water, people, community and culture. Everything that exists around us was here before us and should remain after us.

BEACHES & TOWNS

SOUTH COAST & INLAND

Their new facility includes a detox centre. It's near Chedi Laem Saw.

EAT

HUA THANON MARKET
Thai $

Ban Hua Thanon; 🕐 **6am-6pm;** 🚌
Slip into the rhythm of this village market, a window into the food ways of southern Thailand. Watch the vendors shoo away the flies from the freshly butchered meat and housewives load bundles of vegetables and babies onto the handlebars of motorcycles. Follow the market road to the row of food shops delivering edible southern culture: *kôw mòk gái* (chicken biryani), *kôw yam* (toasted rice with coconut, bean sprouts, lemongrass and dried shrimp) and fiery curries.

NUT'S RESTAURANT *Thai* $
☎ **08 1272 3401; Rd 4170, Thong Krut;** 🕐 **10am-7pm;** 🚶 🦽
One of a string of wooden shacks overlooking Thong Krut's shallow harbour, Nut's is a pleasant spot to sip and nibble a drink and a view of bobby long-tail boats. He's in the midst of a name change but hasn't yet decided upon the restaurant's new moniker.

>WEST COAST

The sunset side of the island is Samui's link to the mainland. Passenger and car ferries discharge their contents at the piers in and around Na Thon, the island's administrative centre.

South of Na Thon, 'civilisation' soon disappears and quaint villages spring up between the coconut plantations and fruit orchards. The bucolic ambience of the west coast is similar to the south coast, but the beaches are better for swimming and strolling, though they don't compare to the postcard beauties of the east coast. For the island cruisers, this area provides a break from the busy east coast, has convivial seafood restaurants and views of offshore Ang Thong National Park.

This is the working side of the island, be it the paper-pushing that occurs in Na Thon or the holiday-making of the Thai tourists from the mainland, arriving aboard the car ferry. Some might boast that the west coast is undiscovered but this would be a stretch considering the number of average hotels and resorts that dot the wide bays around Na Thon.

WEST COAST

◉ SEE
Ban Saket Orchards **1** B4

🏃 DO
Dharma Healing
  International **2** C2

Five Islands Tour.............. **3** B5

🍴 EAT
Big John Seafood **4** B3

🍸 DRINK
Baan Taling Ngam &
  Spa............................... **5** B6
Ban Sabai Sunset Beach
  Resort & Spa................ **6** B5
Five Islands.................. (see **3**)
Nikki Beach.................... **7** B3

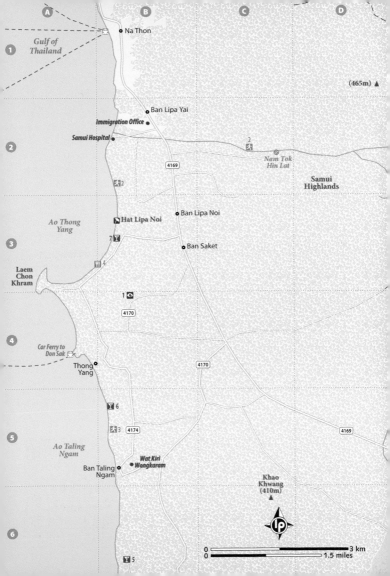

Gulf of
Thailand

Na Thon

(465m) ▲

Ban Lipa Yai

Immigration Office

Samui Hospital

2

Nam Tok
Hin Lat

4169

Samui
Highlands

Ao Thong
Yang

2

Hat Lipa Noi

Ban Lipa Noi

7

Ban Saket

4

Laem
Chon
Khram

1

4170

Car Ferry to
Don Sak

Thong
Yang

4170

4169

6

3

4174

Ao Taling
Ngam

Wat Kiri
Wongkaram

Ban Taling
Ngam

Khao
Khwang
(410m)
▲

5

0   3 km
0   1.5 miles

NA THON

Home to government offices and the big passenger/car ferries, Na Thon hardly factors on most visitors' itinerary except as a ferry waiting room between arrival and departure. The luggage-carrying throngs that unload at Na Thon's pier from the mainland are sorted

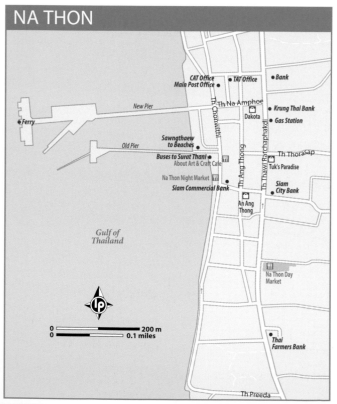

NA THON

CAT Office
Main Post Office
TAT Office
Bank
Th Na Amphoe
New Pier
Th Chonwithi
Krung Thai Bank
Dakota
Gas Station
Ferry
Old Pier
Sawngthaew to Beaches
Buses to Surat Thani
About Art & Craft Cafe
Th Ang Thong
Th Thawi Ratchaphakdi
Th Thorasap
Tuk's Paradise
Na Thon Night Market
Siam Commercial Bank
Siam City Bank
An Ang Thong
Gulf of Thailand
Na Thon Day Market
0 —— 200 m
0 —— 0.1 miles
Thai Farmers Bank
Th Preeda

Wooden shophouses along Thanon Ang Thong

into sŏrng·tăa·ou and whisked away to the various north- and east-coast beaches, hardly taking a second glimpse at this typical Thai town. Far from being beachy, Na Thon does have a few noteworthy aspects – from the Thai markets to low-key cafés – that communicate a much stronger sense of place than the tourist-geared villages of Chaweng and Lamai.

SHOP
DAKOTA
Clothing
☎ 0 7742 0775; Th Na Amphoe, Na Thon;
🕙 10am-6pm; 🚌

The American West has fascinated Thai hippies since the Vietnam War era and has spawned a cottage industry of leatherworkers, like Dakota, who makes tasselled bags, jackets and other cowboy accoutrements.

🏠 THANON ANG THONG
Souvenirs
Na Thon; 🚌 ♿
Step just one block inland from the busy harbour-side road in Na Thon to find this pretty street lined with wooden shophouses, Chinese lanterns and caged singing birds. Souvenir shops of various quality fill the first-floor retail spaces.

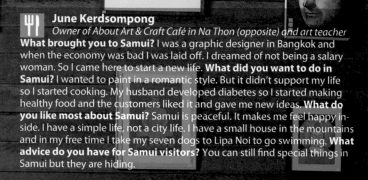

¶¶ June Kerdsompong
Owner of About Art & Craft Café in Na Thon (opposite) and art teacher

What brought you to Samui? I was a graphic designer in Bangkok and when the economy was bad I was laid off. I dreamed of not being a salary woman. So I came here to start a new life. **What did you want to do in Samui?** I wanted to paint in a romantic style. But it didn't support my life so I started cooking. My husband developed diabetes so I started making healthy food and the customers liked it and gave me new ideas. **What do you like most about Samui?** Samui is peaceful. It makes me feel happy inside. I have a simple life, not a city life. I have a small house in the mountains and in my free time I take my seven dogs to Lipa Noi to go swimming. **What advice do you have for Samui visitors?** You can still find special things in Samui but they are hiding.

☐ TUK'S PARADISE
Clothing

☎ 0 7742 0296; Th Thawi Rachaphakdi, Na Thon; ⏰ 9am-6pm; 🚌

Got a suitcase full of clothes that make you sweat in this climate? Go for the gauzy fabrics of Tuk's batik wear. Pick up a few matching outfits from the 2nd floor children's gallery and you'll have pieced together the family cult uniform.

🍴 EAT

🍴 ABOUT ART & CRAFT CAFÉ
Thai & International $$

☎ 08 9724 9673; Th Chonwithi, Na Thon; ⏰ 8am-5pm; Ⓥ

An artistic oasis in the midst of hurried Na Thon, this café serves an eclectic assortment of healthy and wholesome food, gourmet coffee, and, as the name states, art and craft, made by the owner and her friends. Relaxed and friendly, this is also a gathering place for Samui's dwindling population of bohemians and artists.

🍴 NA THON DAY MARKET
Thai $

Th Thawi Rachaphakdi, Na Thon; ⏰ 6am-9pm; 🚌 👶 ♿

This is the biggest and busiest of Samui's fresh markets, selling the usual kitchen goodies as well as takeaway food. On the same side of the street as the 7-Eleven is a row of food shops selling *kôw gaang* (curries served over rice). Keep an eye out for the crispy skinned fried chicken.

🍴 NA THON NIGHT MARKET
Thai $

Th Chonwithi, Na Thon; ⏰ 5pm-midnight; 👶 ♿

Unassuming Na Thon is an uncelebrated sunset destination, best viewed from the night market that sets up near the old pier. Tuck into a plate of *mèe pàt má·prów*, a Samui take on *pàt tai* (Thailand's famous stir-fried noodle dish), as the sun sets over the moored fishing boats.

Fresh produce at Na Thon Day Market

SOUTH OF NA THON

Close to the car ferry pier, the beaches south of Na Thon are a favourite of Thais vacationing from the mainland. Lipa Noi is a pleasant, shallow bay dotted with midrange hotels and resorts that are accustomed to the Thai custom of swimming nearly clothed. Samui residents also feel more comfortable here than at the foreigner-oriented beaches of Chaweng and Lamai. Further south is Taling Ngam, a far-flung roost for the luxury Baan Taling Ngam Resort & Spa.

Beachcombers near Na Thon (p74)

SEE

BAN SAKET ORCHARDS
Rd 4170
Fruit orchards line both sides of the road between the Ring Rd (Rd 4169) and Wat Kiri Wongkaram. Vendors often set up stalls beside the road to sell the ripe fruit fresh off the pregnant boughs.

DO

DHARMA HEALING INTERNATIONAL
☎ 0 7723 4170; www.dharmahealing intl.com; Lipa Yai
There's a cleanse for every class and this Buddhist health retreat offers the island's most intensive and spiritual program. Hillary Hitt, the centre's director, leads fasters through the physical, mental and spiritual journey of cleansing the body and soul. Program treatments include inner-child work, Dharma talks and Vipassana meditation.

FIVE ISLANDS TOUR
☎ 0 7741 5359; www.thefiveislands .com; Five Islands, Taling Ngam; tours from 6500B; ⏰ 10am-12.30pm & 3-5.30pm
The pretty silhouettes of these offshore islands disguises the fact that they are a gold mine, or rather a gold nest. Amid the rocky

> ## LEFT COAST DRINKING
> Watch the day change into night on the sunset side of the island. Cocktails come with scenery at the following west coast resort hotels: **Ban Sabai Sunset Beach Resort & Spa** (☎ 0 7742 8200; Taling Ngam), **Five Islands** (☎ 0 7741 5359; Taling Ngam), **Baan Taling Ngam Resort & Spa** (☎ 0 7742 8200; Taling Ngam).

outcroppings, swiftlets make their nests of twigs and spit, an ingredient that ranks among the world's most expensive animal products. The nests are collected and sent to Chinese markets for the delicacy of bird's-nest soup, renowned for its health benefits. The Five Islands restaurant conducts tours to the islands to learn about the harvesting methods and scramble around the rugged coves. Afterwards a Thai meal is served at the restaurant.

EAT
BIG JOHN SEAFOOD *Thai* *$$*
☎ 0 7742 3025, www.bigjohnsamui.com; Lipa Lovely Beachfront Resort, Lipa Noi; ⏲ 7am-11pm; ♿

Sup with the sunset at friendly Big John's, a popular west coast seafood restaurant. If you've run out of conversation topics, let the live evening entertainment distract you from the silence.

DRINK
NIKKI BEACH *Lounge*
☎ 0 7791 4500; www.nikkibeach.com/kohsamui; Lipa Noi

The acclaimed luxury brand has brought its international *savoir faire* to the secluded west coast of Ko Samui. Expect everything you would from a chic address in St Barts or St Tropez: haute cuisine, chic decor and gaggles of jetsetters.

>NORTH COAST

The north coast is Samui's 'alternative' coast, where commercial development is more subdued and crowds are more discerning and worldly than the east coast. A survivor from Samui's backpacking days, Mae Nam offers the right balance of beach distractions and Thai necessities and is popular with an older European set: practical, frugal, yet slightly adventurous. Because Mae Nam is more affordable, foreign-Thai couples living in Thailand tend to vacation here.

Bo Phut and Fisherman's Village represent the new generation of Thai beaches. The village retains the ambiance of an old fishing town now occupied by design-minded restaurants and hotels. Rarely does commerce in Thailand dress up like this, preferring instead the drab uniform of concrete and neon.

The northwestern peninsula is carved into a few stunning bays for luxury resorts but all can spend the day soaking up the view at the sheltered cove of Ao Thong Sai.

NORTH COAST

◉ SEE

🏃 DO

🍴 EAT

🍸 DRINK

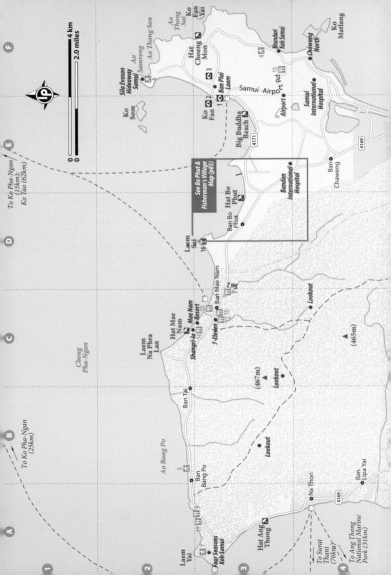

BANG PO & MAE NAM

Bang Po is known for a string of beachfront seafood restaurants, where everyone comes to entertain guests, celebrate a birthday or fritter away the monthly salary. The beach isn't as pretty as Mae Nam's, but it makes an interesting stroll when local Thais comb the shore for cockles or come to bathe the family water buffalo. The public beach access is near Lolita 2 Bungalow on the Ring Rd (Rd 4169).

Mae Nam has the most striking beach on the north coast, fringed with swaying coconut trees, spaced just right for stringing up a hammock. The beach is steeply pitched, good for swimming close to shore, and the water is clear and melodious. Mae Nam town is extraordinarily ordinary with the diurnal tides of Thai life: children being hauled off to school, shopkeepers giving morning alms to monks, and the morning and evening rush to the market. And where there are Thais, there is good food too.

 DO
HEALTH OASIS RESORT
☎ 0 7742 0124; www.healthoasisresort.com; Ring Rd, Bang Po; 🚌 👤
A guesthouse for New Agers, Health Oasis sets itself apart from the island's other health retreats with an on-staff naturopath and herbalist. In addition to fasting and detox programs, it offers ozone therapy, polarity zapper and light transformation. The menu of alternative medicine therapies is available à la carte, and the herbal steam room opens its doors to nonguests from 3pm to 9pm.

SPA AT FOUR SEASONS
www.spafourseasons.com; Four Seasons Koh Samui, Laem Yai; treatments from 3500B; 🕐 9am-9pm
Looking for an excuse to explore this luxury retreat claiming the whole of a rocky peninsula in the northwest corner of the island? Spa treatments have embraced the therapeutic angle – from chakra balancing to ch'i tickling – but the body-wraps stand out as empowering pampering.

 EAT
ANGELA'S BAKERY
International $$
☎ 0 7742 7396; cnr Soi 3 & Ring Rd, Mae Nam; 🕐 8am-6pm; 🚌
Duck through the screen of hanging plants into this beloved bakery, smelling of fresh bread and hospitality. Her sandwiches and cakes have kept many Western expats from wasting away in the land of rice.

🍴 BANG PO SEAFOOD
Thai $$

☎ 0 7742 0010; Ring Rd; ☾ 10am-10pm; 🚌 ♿

More downhome than the other nearby seafood restaurants, Bang Po specialises in everything that is edible from the sea. If you'd rather swim by it than eat it, go for the more pedestrian but delicious whole grilled fish, spiced with coconut milk, turmeric and other seasonings.

🍴 KRUA BANG PO *Thai* $$

☎ 0 7724 7514; Ring Rd, Bang Po; ☾ 10am-10.30pm; 🚌 ♿

One of a string of seafood huts clustered together, Krua Bang Po

Early morning at Mae Nam Market

GRAZING NEAR THE SEVEN

The 7-Eleven convenience stores have inundated the island but they aren't just annoying examples of globalisation. Known as just 'Seven' by the Thais, these quickie marts are useful landmarks and gathering places for food vendors. The 7-Eleven on the western end of Mae Nam is a food beacon: it marks the road leading to the Mae Nam Market (below) and across the street is a shop selling *pàt tai* and *hŏy tôrt* (mussel omelette). Nearby is a vendor who sells *yam ţá·lair* (spicy seafood salad), but you get to pick out the ingredients.

fills the beachside bamboo tables with such local dishes as *nám prík pŏw* (a kind of chili paste) served on a coconut shell and *hèt lúp pàt pèt* (a stir-fried dish containing sea anemone), *yam săh·rài kôr* (seaweed salad) and *ʼboo ním* (deep-fried soft-shell crab mixed with cashews, garlic and pepper).

🍴 MAE NAM MARKET
Thai $

Soi 6, Ring Rd, Mae Nam; ☾ 5.30-9am; 🚌 ♿

This early-morning market, next to a 7-Eleven store, has all the Thai 'eye-openers': thick and sweet coffee, tables of tropical fruits and a famous *kà·nŏm jeen* (rice noodles served with curry) stand to wake up the sinuses.

BEACHES & TOWNS

NORTH COAST

🍴 UNCLE NOI'S
Thai $-$$
Ring Rd, Mae Nam; 🕐 **10.30am-10.30pm;** 🚌 ♿

Just a covered shack, a sizzling wok and a lot of kitchen know-how makes Uncle Noi's a Mae Nam culinary star. Although this is a foreigner-friendly restaurant, curries come with all the required twigs and leaves and none of those dumb-down ingredients, like carrots or cauliflower.

🍸 DRINK
🍸 WOO BAR *Lounge*
4/1 Moo 1 Tambol, Mae Nam; 🕐 **11am-1am**

The W Retreat's signature lobby bar gives the word 'swish' a whole new meaning with cushion-clad pods of seating plunked in the middle of an expansive infinity pool that stretches out over the infinite horizon. This is, without a doubt, the best place on Samui for a sunset cocktail.

BO PHUT & FISHERMAN'S VILLAGE

An anomaly in the Thai islands, Bo Phut's commercial area of Fisherman's Village has more in common with the seaside resorts of Europe than the usual Asian-stye commercial chaos. The village has a pedestrian-friendly main street lined with atmospheric shophouses festooned with bougainvilleas, big picture windows leading to seaside terraces, and caged singing birds, a common adornment along the Malay peninsula. Sophisticated restaurants, bars and boutique hotels now occupy these old houses attracting a cosmopolitan crowd.

Though Bo Phut's beach is not Samui's best, it has become the primary beach for families with small children and the beach road is one of the few areas on the island where you can push a stroller.

🏃 DO
Bo Phut's beach is coarse and shelly with a steep incline into the cloudy water. But the bay is scenic with a wide curve and a view of Ko Pha-Ngan, which protects the bay from seasonal winds and tempers the waves into a gentle surf, making Bo Phut popular with young families and amateur swimmers.

With a mellower vibe than Lamai, Bo Phut has a burgeoning spa and wellness scene that keeps people hanging around longer than the mediocre beach would warrant.

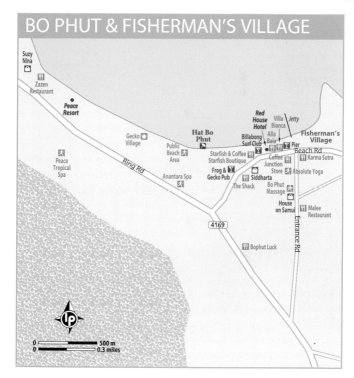

BO PHUT & FISHERMAN'S VILLAGE

Suzy Nina

Zazen Restaurant

Peace Resort

Gecko Village

Public Beach Area

Peace Tropical Spa

Ring Rd

Anantara Spa

Hat Bo Phut

Starfish & Coffee
Starfish Boutique

Frog & Gecko Pub

Red House Hotel

Billabong Surf Club

Villa Bianca   Jetty

Alla Baia   Pier

Fisherman's Village

Beach Rd

Coffee Junction   Karma Sutra

Store   Absolute Yoga

Siddharta

The Shack

Bo Phut Massage

House on Samui   Malee Restaurant

Entrance Rd

4169

Bophut Luck

0 —— 500 m
0 —— 0.3 miles

⚑ ABSOLUTE YOGA

☎ 0 7743 0290; www.absolute
yogasamui.com; Entrance Rd, Fisherman's Village; ☀ classes 10am, 3pm &
6pm; 🚌
Sculpt those unsightly bulges
with a daily dose of hot yoga at
this friendly studio. Need to look
better than good? Try the gentle
fasting and cleansing program,
which does a light house-cleaning.
Yoga lovers often make this a
focus of their Ko Samui vacation
and hang out after class at the
downstairs café. The one-week
introductory promotion costing
1000B is another hook.

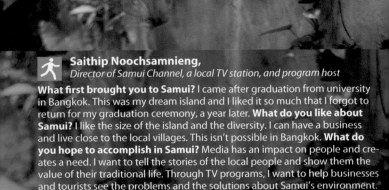

Saithip Noochsamnieng,
Director of Samui Channel, a local TV station, and program host

What first brought you to Samui? I came after graduation from university in Bangkok. This was my dream island and I liked it so much that I forgot to return for my graduation ceremony, a year later. **What do you like about Samui?** I like the size of the island and the diversity. I can have a business and live close to the local villages. This isn't possible in Bangkok. **What do you hope to accomplish in Samui?** Media has an impact on people and creates a need. I want to tell the stories of the local people and show them the value of their traditional life. Through TV programs, I want to help businesses and tourists see the problems and the solutions about Samui's environment. **What do you do with your free time?** I go to my friend's bungalow in Bo Phut and spend time talking, drinking and swimming.

✈ ANANTARA SPA
☎ 0 7742 8300; 99/9 Ring Rd, Bo Phut; treatments 2700-3500B; ⏱ 10am-10pm; 🚌

Renowned and monumental, Anantara Spa creates a fortress against the outside world with lotus ponds and towering Ayuthaya-style architecture. The spa's focus is on Ayurvedic treatments like *shirodhara,* in which warm oil is massaged over the forehead, or 'third' eye, a surprisingly tense part of the body.

✈ BO PHUT MASSAGE
☎ 0 87976 0869; Entrance Rd, Fisherman's Village; massages 250B; ⏱ 10am-9pm; 🚌 ♿

Once the beach massage ladies have gone home, whatever is a twisted up traveller to do? Try an evening massage at this Wat Pho certified shop set in a traditional wooden house.

✈ PEACE TROPICAL SPA
☎ 0 7743 0199; Ring Rd, Bo Phut; treatments 1800-3000B; ⏱ 10am-10pm; 🚌

For the frugal spa fanatics, Peace Tropical Spa has a lovely garden setting and prices that aren't too luxurious. Its other asset is a tiled jet-pool big enough to dog paddle in. It is across from Peace Resort.

✈ PUBLIC BEACH AREA
Beach Rd, btwn Shades Restaurant & Smile House; 🚌 ♿

TIMING THE TIDE
Due to its proximity to the equator, the tidal range in the Gulf of Thailand varies only slightly, often by no more than 3m. During the summer months, especially July and August, the tides are higher than in the winter, and the difference between low tide and high tide can vary by as little as 5cm, making it appear as if there is only one tide per day.

If you're a foreigner, any stretch of sand is open to you. But local Thais tend to be more cautious and stick to the undeveloped spots. This shady area is Bo Phut's most communal stretch: families lay down beach mats and sand toys, tired sarong-sellers catch a few winks and the hungry shuffle over to the nearby *sôm đam* (papaya salad) stand for a taste of Isan.

🛍 SHOP
Fisherman's Village is fertile shopping ground for funky and fresh women's clothing, imported from Chiang Mai, Bali and Nepal. So don't stress over packing, just buy it once you get here.

🛍 COFFEE JUNCTION STORE
Clothing
☎ 08 9866 1085; Beach Rd, Fisherman's Village; ⏱ 8am-10pm; 🚌

If you've exhausted your souvenir tolerance with far too many factory-made chotchke, go local at this small shop tucked nicely into the far end of this main street café. Pick up a few coconut-based body products made by Samui's very own Simply Samui company.

HOUSE ON SAMUI Clothing

☎ 0 7724 5082; 38/1 Entrance Rd, Fisherman's Village; 🕓 12.30-10.30pm; 🚌
For wash-and-wear gals and guys, these natural cotton clothes come from Thailand's textile capital of Chiang Mai and will put the flower child back into your wardrobe.

SIDDHARTA Clothing

☎ 0 7724 5014; Beach Rd, Fisherman's Village; 🕓 10am-9pm; 🚌
A French import company brings its globetrotting treasures from Bali and Nepal to the shores of Samui. The racks are filled with cool geometric beach cover-ups and flower appliqué skirts –

fashionable replacements, if you grow tired of the contents of your suitcase.

STARFISH BOUTIQUE Clothing

☎ 0 7742 7201; 51/7 Beach Rd, Fisherman's Village; 🕓 11.30am-10.30pm; 🚌
More trendsetting than trendy, the boutique arm of this restaurant-café dares to be flamboyant with fashion bearing a Bangkok pedigree.

SUZY NINA Décor

☎ 0 7724 5221; www.suzynina.com; 3/3 Ring Rd, West Bo Phut; 🕓 11am-9pm; 🚌
Samui's answer to Pier One, this interior design shop sells ethno-chic interiors, but is best known for its silk and natural cotton bed-linens and custom-made drapes. Finger through the fabric room loaded with elegant Thai and Burmese silks.

SAVING THE COCONUT

The versatile coconut has shaped the fortunes and culture of the island. It was Samui's first export commodity and factors into almost every local dish. But today coconut farms are more profitable as residential villas and hotels, and some wonder when Samui will begin importing its once iconic crop. Hoping to preserve the remaining coconut farms and its traditional way of life, entrepreneurs Shelagh Foster and Sannit Viriyanon have found yet another application of the coconut: as a natural ingredient in health and beauty products. Their company, Simply Samui (www.simplysamui.com), uses Samui-grown and -processed coconut oil in scrubs, lip balms and massage oil that are sold at shops and pharmacies throughout the island. You can also try its spa line developed especially for Hideaway Spa at Sila Evason (p94).

🍴 EAT

Take your appetite out for a stroll through Fisherman's Village to join the other well-dressed diners flipping through the menus of Italian, French, Thai and even Scandinavian restaurants. In any other neighbourhood, we'd sniff at these foreign imports but Bo Phut does international food with more flair.

🍴 ALLA BAIA *Italian* $$-$$$

☎ 0 7724 5566; 49/1 Beach Rd, Fisher-man's Village; ⏱ 6-11pm; 🚌

A crisp seaside spot with white tablecloths provides a smart canvas to show off your newly acquired suntan and sup on handmade ravioli and exuberant salads. Skip the mediocre pizzas for another glass of wine; you're on holiday after all.

🍴 BOPHUT LUCK
International $

☎ 08 7283 6528; Ring Rd; ⏱ 9am-6pm; 🚌 Ⓥ ♿

With a few cold cases and a big grin from Noi, Bophut Luck supplies Samui restaurants with homemade yogurt, feta cheese and sour cream. You can cut out the middleman with a visit to this bare-bones shop – a common morning ritual for Bo Phut veterans.

🍴 COFFEE JUNCTION
International $-$$

☎ 08 9866 1085; Beach Rd, Fisherman's Village; ⏱ 8am-10pm; 🚌

Good coffee shops not only know how to brew, they also have a front-row view of folks who are more active than their customers. Planted in front of the pier, Coffee Junction provides an open window on the crossroads into Fisherman's Village, perfect for people-watching.

🍴 KARMA SUTRA
International $$

☎ 0 7742 5198; www.karmasutra.org; Beach Rd, Fisherman's Village; ⏱ breakfast, lunch & dinner

A haze of purples and pillows, this charming chow spot in the heart of Bo Phut's Fisherman's Village serves up international and Thai eats listed on colourful chalkboards. Karma Sutra doubles as a clothing boutique.

🍴 MALEE RESTAURANT
Thai $

Entrance Rd, Fisherman's Village; ⏱ 11am-10pm; 🚌 Ⓥ

For all of its charms, Fisherman's Village is somewhat lean on local Thai food shops. Graded on this curve, Malee Restaurant is a stand-out for its downhome ambience, where you can rub shoulders with locals and have the street noise

BEACHES & TOWNS

NORTH COAST

drowned out by blaring Thai music videos. Her menu is easy even if the dishes do lack a bit of punch.

🍽 SHACK
International $$

☎ 0 7724 5041; Beach Rd, Fisherman's Village; 🕑 11am-2pm & 6pm-midnight; 🚌 ♿

This is a brawny contender among a clique of pretty girl restaurants. The Shack is all about the grill, which gets front and centre attention. Steaks and seafood spit and sizzle on the open flame and then fill up a hungryman's plate alongside an array of salads and dipping sauces.

🍽 STARFISH & COFFEE
Thai $-$$$

☎ 0 7742 7201; Beach Rd, Fisherman's Village; 🕑 11am-11pm; 🚌 Ⓥ

Young and fun, this seaside restaurant creates a clubby vibe with an ambient soundtrack and a luscious diva interior. Although the Thai food is just a notch above guesthouse fare, it is affordable, an unstylish concept in this stylish village.

🍽 VILLA BIANCA *Italian* $$

☎ 0 7724 5041; Beach Rd, Fisherman's Village; 🕑 lunch & dinner

Another fantastic spot on Samui serving delicious Italian and international cuisine, Villa Bianca is a

The stylish interior of Starfish & Coffee

sea of crisp white tablecloths and woven lounge chairs. Who knew wicker could be so sexy?

🍴 ZAZEN RESTAURANT
Thai & International $$$

☎ 0 7743 0345; www.samuizazen.com; Zazen Boutique Resort & Spa, Ring Rd, Bo Phut; ⏰ 11am-11pm; 🚌

Bathed in the music of the ocean and the soft red glow of lanterns, romantic Zazen has created a sophisticated setting for Samui's gastronomic visitors. The menu is a global scrapbook of dishes, totalling close to 100 items and drawing from every imaginable world cuisine. Take your time in reading through the tome or surrender to the discovery menus that make the choices for you.

🍸 DRINK

Fisherman's Village has a lively bar scene – from grey-haired pubs to sleek fortnighter clubs – but it knows its limits. Places close up at 11pm giving you just enough time to gulp enough drinks for a good night's sleep. If you want drunken abandon, head to Chaweng.

🍸 BILLABONG SURF CLUB
Bar

☎ 0 7743 0144; Beach Rd, Fisherman's Village; ⏰ 6-11pm

Finding your compatriots is easy

WHINING ABOUT WINE
Thailand isn't kind to wine drinkers. The government slaps a 400% tax on the imported beverage. The hot climate beats up delicate French wines and the humidity makes the boisterous reds almost unpalatable. But dedication to the drink persists and most upscale restaurants do their best to offer well-rounded wine lists. To avoid a glass of vinegar, though, go for sturdier wines that can take tropical temperatures and order from places that have dedicated wine storage areas (even for reds). Or bow to the climate and order a glass of white, Ms Priss.

in Fisherman's Village: there's a pub for every nationality. Aussies segregate themselves at this sports bar for suds, pies and the match.

🍸 FROG & GECKO PUB
Bar

☎ 0 7742 5248; Beach Rd, Fisherman's Village; ⏰ 11am-11pm

Tie on your thinking cap for this English pub's popular Wednesday quiz night. On other nights, it is a low-key spot to swap tall tales and big fish stories.

🍸 PIER *Bar*

☎ 0 7743 0681; Beach Rd, Fisherman's Village; ⏰ 6-11pm

The cocktail crowd populates this slick multi-level monument to

REEF RESEARCH

Once you master breathing through a tube, help the world's scientists monitor the health of the reefs in the Gulf of Thailand. The CoralWatch program (www.coralwatch.org), sponsored by PADI, collects data from divers about coral health and bleaching. Dive shops can provide colour charts that are used to match and map the colour of the coral, an indication of the colonies' health.

glass and steel designed by Thai architect Duangrit Bunnag, whose other project includes trendy H1 complex in Bangkok. Wave at Ko Pha-Ngan from.the seaside terrace or just contemplate being cultured and fabulous.

 PLAY
GECKO VILLAGE
Club

☎ 0 7724 5554; www.geckosamui.com; Beach Rd, Bo Phut

For electronica fans, Gecko Village is the original maven of beats. It's a beachfront bar and resort that has used its London connections to lure international DJs to Samui paradise. The New Year's Eve parties and Sunday sessions are now legend thanks to the big names that grace the turntables.

BIG BUDDHA BEACH & CHOENG MON

The northeastern finger of Samui has various aliases, but most refer to the western side as Big Buddha Beach (or Bangrak) and the eastern side as Choeng Mon. Big Buddha Beach is on the flight path and is better for watching fishing boats than bobbing in the sea. Its greatest asset is its boat pier, the most convenient link between Chaweng and ferries to Ko Pha-Ngan and Ko Tao.

On the sunrise side, Ao Thong Sai is a picturesque bay surrounded by high cliffs and Samui's first luxury resort, Tongsai Bay, which pioneered this isolated corner. The beach still has a frontier feel and families with young children appreciate the calm water and low-key energy.

 SEE
PLAI LAEM FISH MARKET
Rd 4171, Ban Plai Laem; ⏲ 5-9pm
Muslim fisherfolk unload their catch at this very busy fish market. The place is crammed with eagle-eyed housewives and discerning chefs who hail from Samui's restaurants.

Stare in amazement at the 18-armed Buddha statue at Wat Plai Laem

⊙ WAT PHRA YAI

Rd 4171, Big Buddha Beach; donations accepted; ⏲ 6am-6pm

Big Buddha Beach's eponymous temple boasts a 12m-high Buddha figure seated on a small promontory known as Ko Fan. It was built in 1972 and surveys a scene of moored fishing boats and overhead flying boats. An attached souvenir village signals the unabashed mixing of religion and commerce.

⊙ WAT PLAI LAEM

Rd 4171, Ban Plai Laem; donations accepted; ⏲ 6am-6pm

This little temple has several large attractions: three gigantic depictions of Buddha set in a man-made lake. The centrepiece is an 18-armed Hindu-style Buddha next to a lotus blossom and a fat, Chinese-style Buddha. Considered an act of merit, Thai Buddhists, especially the young ones, feed the hungry fish, who live a charmed life in the surrounding lake. Sometimes this temple is called Wat Laem Suan Naram.

🏃 DO

🏃 ABSOLUTE SANCTUARY

☎ 0 7760 1190; www.absolutesanct uary.com; Beach Rd, Choeng Mon; detox programs from 15,500B

The newcomer to the health scene, Absolute Sanctuary is

expanding on its success with its Bo Phut yoga studio with this detox resort. To distinguish itself from Samui's free-form health centres, Absolute is for the absolutely certain fasters who want a strict, medically supervised regimen coupled with a full menu of yoga classes. And because this is your vacation, such dedication need only last three days or so.

HIDEAWAY SPA

☎ 0 7724 5678; www.sixsenses.com; **Sila Evason Hideaway Samui, Laem Samrong; treatments 2500-5000B**
Allowing the natural world to provide the splendour, the spa at Sila Evason is perched among the rock cliffs of the island's northeast promontory, practically kissing offshore Ko Pha-Ngan. Signature therapies combine Western and Eastern massage techniques as well as the house spa products made locally by Simply Samui.

🍴 EAT

🍴 BBC *International* $$

☎ 0 7742 5089; www.bbcrestaurant.com; **Big Buddha Beach;** ☽ **breakfast, lunch & dinner**
No, this place has nothing to do with *Doctor Who* – BBC stands for Big Buddha Café. It's popular with

the local expats, the international menu is large, and there are exquisite ocean views from the patio.

🍴 DINING ON THE ROCKS
Pan-Asian $$$

☎ 0 7724 5678; **Sila Evason Hideaway Samui, Laem Samrong;** ☽ **6-10pm**
The restaurant is named literally: it is little more than a series of wooden decks with the deep ocean below and the stars winking above. A dramatic setting with an equally dramatic menu of nouveau-Asian confections, such as avocado mousse and mango salsa paired with salmon. Some of the herbs and vegetables that grace the plates have been harvested from the hotel's garden.

🍴 RAN KUAYTIAW LEUK LAP
Thai $

Samui Airport Rd, Choeng Mon; ☽ **11am-3pm**
Looking like the 'Cousin It' of noodle shops, Mystery Noodles is shielded from the road by a curtain of greenery. Duck inside to find a few busy tables filled with Thai hotel workers and steaming bowls of *đôm yam mŏo* (pork noodles in a spicy broth). Another local favourite are the meaty *lôok chín* (pork balls) that taste like generic hot dogs to us.

>ISLAND HOPPING

Island hop through Ang Thong National Marine Park (p96)

ANG THONG NATIONAL PARK

Take a day trip to Ang Thong National Park, a primordial landscape of humpbacked limestone islands covered in scraggly beard-like vegetation, anchored in the deep blue sea.

The park covers a total area of 102 sq km (with land comprising only 18 sq km) and used to be a training ground for the Royal Thai Navy. The park is 35km west of Samui. About 82% of the total archipelago is protected as national park. The best time to visit is in February, March and April, when the seas are relatively calm. During November and December, the monsoon rains make the seas too rough to visit.

Ko Wua Talap (Sleeping Cow Island) is the largest island in the chain and hosts the national park office and visitor bungalows. The island has a stunning mountain-top viewpoint, a necessary reward after clawing your way to the top of the 450m trail, booby-trapped with sharp jagged rocks. A second trail leads to Tham Bua Bok, a cavern with lotus-shaped stalagmites and stalactites. There's a small sandy beach on the sunrise side of the island and a general castaway's tranquillity.

Sail around the island cliffs in Ang Thong National Park

But the myth-maker is **Ko Mae** (Mother Island) and its inner lagoon (*tá·lair nai*). The exterior of the island is a jagged shell of limestone and grizzled vegetation but a steep climb up to the top reveals a sink hole filled with a gleaming gem-coloured lake, filled by underwater channels. You can look but you can't touch; the lagoon is strictly off-limits to the unclean human body.

The naturally occurring stone arches on **Ko Samsao** and **Ko Tai Plao** are visible during seasonal tides and weather conditions. Because the sea is quite shallow around the island chain, reaching a maximum depth of 10m, extensive coral reefs have not developed, except in a few protected pockets on the southwest and northeast sides. There's a shallow coral reef near Ko Tai Plao and Ko Samsao that has decent, but not excellent, snorkelling. There are also several novice dives for exploring shallow caves and colourful coral gardens and spotting banded sea snakes and turtles. Soft powder beaches line **Ko Tai Plao**, **Ko Wuakantang** and **Ko Hintap**.

Most visitors come on an organised day tour from Samui. Tour operators are plentiful and offer a standard itinerary: two-hour transport from Samui to the park, kayaking and snorkelling, hikes, lunch and return transport. Other islands might be included depending on the weather. These tours are mainly sightseeing trips with some exertion built in. The hike to peek in at Ko Mae's inner lagoon is steep and breaks more than a sweat. The kayaking segment runs an obstacle course through a cluster of tight-knit islands and puts paddlers at eye-level with the crabs and oysters demarcating the high-water mark.

For a more intimate exploration of Ang Thong, consider an overnight stay at one of the park-operated bungalows on Ko Wua Talap or other island campsites. As the forest wakes and prepares for bed, you're more likely to see the island's full-time residents – birds and monkeys. Tour companies can provide transport from and to Samui, if you plan on overnighting. There's also a restaurant on the island, but you might want to bring some extras supplies, especially bug juice.

FAST FACTS

Getting There & Away The only transport to Ang Thong is by tour operators from Ko Samui.

Park Admission adult/child 400/200B, sometimes included in tour packages.

Tours from Ko Samui Blue Star Kayaking (p41)

Information & Accommodation Park headquarters (☎ 0 7728 6025; www.dnp.go.th; Ko Wua Talap; r 500-1400B)

KO PHA-NGAN

Goldilocks would be pleased to find Ko Pha-Ngan: it isn't too small, too developed or too far-flung. It sits perfectly between the extremes and has a beach for every type of traveller: from the Full Moon partiers to the family of four. The island is carved into sandy coves with offshore reefs on the west coast and a thick jungle crown that can be explored on elephant treks or waterfall hikes.

If Chaweng could have a protégé, it would be **Hat Rin**, a long sandy cape along the southern coast. During the famous Full Moon Party, crowds arrive en masse to gulp down their weight in buckets, gesticulate to techno and gawk at the fire dancers. Though it is known as a trippy rave scene, the Full Moon is more of a drunk fest with a thumping baseline. If you're a Full Moon virgin, you can skip across the sea from Samui for the night and be home in time for the sunrise.

For something quieter, disperse to the east or west coasts. Visiting the east coast is a deep immersion into beach seclusion because it is accessible only by boat from Hat Rin or along unpaved jungle paths. Most east coast devotees set down roots as it is hard to come and go quickly. More

Be dazzled by the fire dancers at Ko Pha-Ngan's Full Moon Party

KO PHA-NGAN

GULF OF
THAILAND

Ao Hat
Thong Lang
Hat Thong
Lang
Ko Ma
(Horse Island)
Ban Mae
Hat
Ao Mae Hat
Ao
Chalok
Lam
Hat
Khom
Laem
Kung Yai
Hat Khuat
(Bottle Beach)
Khao
Kin Non
(440m)
Hat Thong Nai Pan Noi
Nam Tok
Wang Sai
(Paradise Falls)
Hat Salat
Ban Chalok
Lam
Ban Fai Mai
Ao Thong
Nai Pan Noi
Ao Hat Salat
Hat Yao
Ban Wang
Ta Khian
Khao Ra
(620m)
Nam Tok
Than Prawet
Ao Thong Nai Pan Yai
Hat Thong
Nai Pan Yai
Ban Thong
Nai Pan
Hat Chaophao
Ko Kong
Than Sadet
Laem Son
Ban Si Thanu
Khao
Ta Luang
(476m)
378m
Hat Sadet
Ao Thong
Reng
Ao Si
Thanu
Ban Hin
Kong
Ban Madeua
Wan
Ban
Thong
Nang
Nam Tok
Than Sadet
Ban Nam
Tok
Ao Hin
Kong
498m
Nam Tok
Than Prapat
Ao Wok Tum
Ban Wok
Tum
Nam Tok
Phaeng
Ko Pha-Ngan
Hospital
525m
Hat Yang
Ao Nai Wok
Wat
Khao
Tham
Hat Yao
Ko Tae Nai
Pier
Thong
Sala
Ban Nok
Hat Wai
Nam
Laem
Klang
Ao Bang
Charu
Ban Tai
Ban Khai
Pang Bon
Hat Thian
Hat Yuan
To Ko Samui
(Na Thon;
25km)
Hat Rin Nok
(Sunrise Beach)
Hat Rin Nai
(Sunset Beach)
Laem
Hat Rin

0 ——— 5 km
0 ——— 3 miles

To Big Buddha
Beach (Ko
Samui; 15km)

FAST FACTS

Getting There & Away Daily boats leave from Samui's Mae Nam, Big Buddha Beach and Na Thon piers (one hour, 220B to 250B). Ko Pha-Ngan's main pier is at Thong Sala but some ferries go directly to Hat Rin. During the Full Moon Party, boats leave from Big Buddha Beach to Hat Rin (30 minutes, 500B) every hour from 7am to midnight and return every hour from 3am to 7am.
Getting Around Chartered sŏrng·tǎa·ou and water taxi.
Information Backpackers Information Center (☎ 0 7737 5535; backpackersthailand.com; Soi Sea Garden, Hat Rin Nok)
Accommodation High Life (☎ 0 7734 9114; Hat Yao; www.highlifebungalow.com; r 500-2000B); Plaa's Than Sadet (☎ 0 7744 5191; Than Sadet; r 500B); Cookies Bungalows (☎ 0 7734 9125; Hat Salat; r 1200-2400B)

restless types prefer the west coast, which is connected to the port town of Thong Sala by sealed road.

In the northern nook, **Ao Thong Nai Pan** is divided into two bays with lots of cove appeal. Since it takes some trouble to get here, no-one leaves for a change of scenery, they just scope out the next best place to stay. There are also a few necessities if you haven't yet learned to live off the land.

Heading south, **Ao Thong Reng** has been honoured by several royal visits and could easily qualify as having heavenly beaches, including **Hat Sadet**. There's a small altar of sand for worshipping the contours of the undulating coast and the shimmering sea. In the interior is **Nam Tok Than Sadet**, which cascades between boulders before plunging into a forested pool. Day-trippers come from other parts of the island to admire the cascade.

Hat Thian hosts the **Sanctuary & Wellness Centre** (☎ 08 1271 3614; www .thesanctuary-kpg.com), a legend in old backpacking circles where the hippie hobbies of yoga, detox and veggie food still rule. The biggest mane of sand on this coast is at **Hat Yuan**, now sprouting a few boutique resorts for castaways with cash.

If you need a splash of sociability with your scenery, opt for the west coast. One of the longest beaches, **Hat Yao** stretches for close to 1km. The bay is shallow and popular with families. At night, the beach is lit with barbecues and low-key beer swilling. **Hat Salat** has swimming, snorkelling and sleepy island vibes with a sprinkle of creature comforts. Further north, **Ao Mae Hat** is a fishing bay leashed to **Ko Ma**, an offshore island with good snorkelling. Descending into the valley around Ban Chalok Lam, you can catch a boat to **Hat Khuat** (Bottle Beach) on the north coast. The golden sands and mountain backdrop are all the entertainment most visitors want.

KO TAO

If Samui is the 'big city' of the archipelago, then Ko Tao is the country cousin. Turtle Island is the smallest of the island chain and the least developed, but it does compete with its flamboyant neighbours thanks to its reputation as a dive mecca. Just offshore are colourful coral reefs teeming with marine life and within a few minutes' boat ride are top-notch dive sites. The ease and the affordability of diving on the island makes it unique among the world's dive centres.

If you are making the hop from Samui specifically for diving, most schools offer package deals that include accommodation. Expect crowds between December and April and immediately following a Full Moon Party on Ko Pha-Ngan. Snorkelling is also widespread on the island and it is easy to rent equipment and charter a fishing boat to hit the most popular spots, mainly on the east coast. (For more information on diving and snorkelling in Ko Tao, see p22.)

On shore, Ko Tao's coarse sand beaches can't compete with Samui's voluptuous coastline. But what it lacks in powder, it makes up for in ambiance. The island is still a hammock-hangers dream, which will seem straight out of the backpacker days of the 1970s compared to the new millennium

Stretch out on Ko Tao's longest beach, Hat Sai Ri (p103)

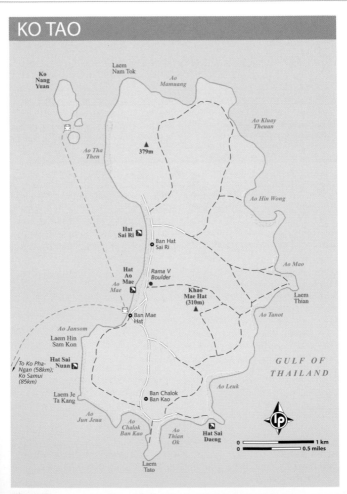

KO TAO

Ko Nang Yuan

Laem Nam Tok

Ao Mamuang

Ao Kluay Theuan

Ao Tha Then

379m

Ao Hin Wong

Hat Sai Ri

Ban Hat Sai Ri

Ao Mao

Hat Ao Mae

Rama V Boulder

Ao Mae

Khao Mae Hat (310m)

Laem Thian

Ban Mae Hat

Ao Tanot

Ao Jansom

Laem Hin Sam Kon

GULF OF THAILAND

To Ko Pha-Ngan (58km); Ko Samui (85km)

Hat Sai Nuan

Laem Je Ta Kang

Ban Chalok Ban Kao

Ao Leuk

Ao Jun Jeua

Ao Chalok Ban Kao

Ao Thian Ok

Hat Sai Daeng

0   1 km
0   0.5 miles

Laem Tato

FAST FACTS

Getting There & Away Daily ferries leave from Samui's Mae Nam, Big Buddha Beach and Na Thon ports (1½ hours, 350B to 600B) with a stop in Ko Pha-Ngan.

Getting Around Chartered sŏrng·tăa·ou (converted pick-up truck).

Information Koh Tao Online (kohtaoonline.com)

Tours from Ko Samui Dive trips available through Samui International Diving School (p42) and Discovery Divers (p41)

Accommodation Hin Wong Bungalows (☎ 0 7745 6006, Ao Hin Wong; r 300-400B); Mango Bay Grand Resort (☎ 0 7745 6097; Mango Bay; r 1400-3000B); Charm Churee Villa (☎ 0 7745 6393; Ao Jansom; r 3200-12,200B)

energy of Samui. There is one paved road that runs northwest from the pier. Every other route is basically a drainage ditch through the jungle.

Hat Sai Ri is the island's longest stretch of beach (which can't hold a grain of sand to Chaweng) and is the nexus for the island's dive industry. It is filled with a young crowd that pushes off early for dive trips and decompresses in the open-air bars to compare big fish tales. On the south coast, **Ao Chalok Ban Kao** is another convergence of commercial congestion on a much smaller beach.

If you've just come to 'take a break' from Samui, disappear into the jungle and emerge on the eastern side of the island where you can go cove hunting. The big kahuna of the east coast is the boulder strewn beach of **Ao Hin Wong**. The rounded rocks part slightly for a welcome mat of sand and then plunge into the clear blue waters where little fish will nibble at your toes. This is a popular snorkelling and dive spot.

To the north of Hin Wong, the shallow bay of **Ao Mamuang** (Mango Bay) is ideal for water sports: scuba, snorkelling, kayaking and swimming. The bay is also Ko Tao's emerging upscale destination for the beyond-bungalow crowd.

Further south is **Laem Thian**, a pretty view-engrossing cape with an offshore reef and a hard-to-reach, hard-to-leave ambience. The rocky bay at **Ao Tanot** knits together jungle, sea and sky, but most agree that **Ao Leuk** has the prettiest pitch of sand.

Once you've adjusted to the lonely east coast, you might need even more seclusion. **Ko Nang Yuan**, just off the northwest coast, is a private island with one resort and no land access. Boats from Mae Hat and Hat Sai Ri make the journey for snorkelling day-trippers, who must pay a 100B admission fee.

There's more to Samui than the beaches so bring along your walking shoes for island expeditions, shopping outings, food scouting and bar hopping. Families will be thoroughly entertained with elephant rides, butterfly parks and the odd sights of a Thai marketplace.

Set Chaweng's copy artists to work to re-create that masterpiece you've always wanted (p43)

SNAPSHOTS

ACCOMMODATION

Samui sleeps mainly in resort hotels: minicities with multistorey hotel rooms and stand-alone villas, restaurants, a pool and, in some cases, spas and bars. Most resorts are locally owned and managed, an unusual economic paradigm in an international destination. And in some cases the hotel sits on land that has been in the family for generations. The foreign investors are arriving with their global brands, but the prime real estate has already been developed, leaving substandard beaches to be augmented by ultra-luxury lodging. In these cases, the beach is just a scenic backdrop not an attraction. Reflecting global hotel trends, design is starting to dominate over amenities or size. Boutique hotels have scaled back their footprint and often have artsy villas with their own pools. In a few pockets of the island, you'll still find backpacker-style bungalows, but these are a rare breed.

Compared to other Thai beaches, prices on Samui look a lot like the First World. There are three pricing seasons: high (December to April), middle (July to September) and low (October and November). If you've entertained the idea of a Samui vacation, then it is probably during a peak period: Christmas, winter in northern Europe, Chinese New Year and Easter. The lowest period is during the wettest part of the monsoon season (October to November). On Chaweng the difference between high season and low season rates is anywhere from 500B to 3000B.

Being the prettiest and most popular beach, Chaweng charges the most for the privilege of staying here. Package tourists, families with older children and partying 20-somethings are the primary clientele.

Eat at Page Restaurant (p47), a good excuse to then explore the ultra-austere Library Resort

Central Chaweng is the busiest part of the beach and has the nearly-all-night party. If you aren't going to be at the bars listening to techno, think about staying at the quieter southern end near Chaweng Noi or in North Chaweng.

Once known for its cheapie bungalows, Chaweng has only a few survivors for the late-to-bed crowd and they start at 1500B (hardly cheap) in the high season. The rest of the beach is populated by resorts with detached villas in jungle-filled gardens or no-nonsense hotel rooms. And a few concept hotels, like Library or Poppies, are starting to introduce thematic lodging. For midrange places, expect to pay around 5000B in high season, and around 10,000B for top-enders.

Lamai is a little cheaper, a little smaller and the clientele is a little rougher than Chaweng. Or better put: Chaweng is for frat boys, Lamai for biker dudes. As for accommodation, Lamai has a little of everything: sprawling resorts, mom-and-pop bungalows and a few new-style boutiques. The bungalows near Hin Ta Hin Yai are still affordable (around 700B in high season) and full of rustic beach charm. Expect to pay 2500B to 3000B for midrange hotels and 5500B to 8500B for top end. Prices in Lamai are about the standard for the rest of the island.

While the south and west coasts are very charming areas for 'real' Samui, the beaches are not Samui's best and they are far from necessities, such as restaurants and shops. Both coasts have, or will soon have, top-end self-contained resorts that act as independent cities. Otherwise you'll need to rent a vehicle (and deal with the erratic traffic) or pay for the overpriced taxis (which could cost 1000B for one round-trip outing).

Mae Nam has some modest, but perfectly poised, shacks on the beach with the sound of the ocean as the primary amenity. There are also a few grown-up resorts. Bo Phut and Fisherman's Village are all the rage for boutique hotel fans, honeymooners and the eccentric elite. Choeng Mon has an interesting mix of chi-chi resorts and humble huts that peacefully share the beach and a laid-back attitude. All but Choeng Mon are well-situated for journeys to other parts of the island.

If you're looking for long-term lodging or private villas, you're in luck: Samui is over-run with properties for rent. Most are along the north or south coast. **Sawadee.com** (www.sawadee.com) is the island's primary online booking agent for hotels and rental properties and includes reviews from former guests.

Stay and eat at the quirky Red House Hotel (p109), Fisherman's Village

BEST FOR FAMILIES
> Mae Nam Resort (Mae Nam; www
  .maenamresort.com)
> Peace Resort (Bo Phut; www.peace
  resort.com)
> Rocky Resort (south coast; www
  .rockyresort.com)
> Centara Grand Beach Resort Samui
  (pictured above; Chaweng; www
  .centarahotelsresorts.com)

BEST FOR HONEYMOONERS
> Sila Evason Hideaway & Spa
  (Laem Samrong; www.sixsenses
  .com)
> Bhundari Koh Samui (North Chaweng;
  www.bhundhari.com)
> Zazen Boutique Resort & Spa (Bo Phut;
  www.samuizazen.com)

BEST FOR BACKPACKERS
> Paradise Bungalow (Lamai; www
  .nojbarparadise.com)
> Shangri-la (Mae Nam; www.geocities
  .com/pk_shangrilah/)
> Ark Bar Guesthouse (Chaweng; www
  .ark-bar.com)

QUIRKIEST HOTELS
> Jungle Club (Chaweng Noi; sawadee
  .com)
> AKWA Guesthouse (Chaweng; www
  .akwaguesthouse.com)
> Red House Hotel (Bo Phut; www
  .design-visio.com)

BARS & CLUBS

Samui aspires to be an Ibiza party scene and occasionally it delivers with a high-powered DJ and crowd of writhing bodies. But most nights, the party scene is beachy and boozey with a little port town seediness thrown in.

Samui feeds the house heads with close proximity to Ko Pha-Ngan's monthly Full Moon Party (p98), the original beach rave. Party promoters and boat operators make it easy to jump over to Ko Pha-Ngan for the night and return to Samui before sun-up.

To keep the party people on Samui's shores, it has invented its own lunar events: Black Moon and Escape parties (see Party Moon, p51). Sunday gigs and a famous New Year's Eve party are held at Gecko Village (p92) in Bo Phut. Weekend nights, DJ fans make the trek to Q Bar Samui (p52), Samui's most cosmo club. On Wednesday nights, the beach bars in Chaweng corral the crowds on the sand with house-music parties.

But every other night, night-crawlers are in central Chaweng Beach Rd following an age-old migration pattern: evening buckets at Ark Bar (p49) and then on to the bars and clubs that line Soi Solo and Soi Green Mango. Chaweng stays up until 2am and some venues keep the good times rolling until 6am.

And where there is neon in Thailand, there are *gà-teu·i* (ladyboys), who are either cross-dressers or transgendered, and assume a flamboyant feminine persona. Ladyboy cabarets flourish in Chaweng and Lamai and feature feather boas and synchronised stage shows with varying degrees of cheesiness. (We've also heard that a ladyboy volleyball team practises on the beach in Chaweng most evenings before they don their sequins and heels.)

Throughout Chaweng, there's plenty of sloppy behaviour and drunken abandon, an environment in which opportunists flourish. In the past, Samui has suffered many smudges to its reputation as a tropical paradise after foreigners were attacked and even killed during late-night ragers. Remember that there is economic disparity on this island and exercise 'street smarts' even on the beach.

For a more subdued crowd, watching the sunset with a liquid companion is another Samui speciality. Sunset drinks are served wherever there are thirsty people – but mainly at beachside bars and hill-top restaurants across the island. The west coast claims the unobstructed sunset view and caters especially to this important part of cocktail hour but the view is just as fine on the east coast where the sand turns golden as the sun slips away. Though it has neither a sunset view nor a beach location, Tropical Murphy's (p50) is another pre-dinner watering hole that manages to put everyone in a good mood.

Lamai and Bo Phut have a few bars and clubs but none that can counteract the magnetic forces of Chaweng's. Mae Nam's party scene is pretty lacklustre. The access roads to the beach boast some depressing hostess bars and the beach guesthouses often don't even turn on the ubiquitous fairy lights.

The bar menu in Thailand includes the local beers Singha (pronounced 'sing') and Chang (meaning 'elephant') and imported lagers like Heineken. Familiar cocktails, like Kamikazes and Screwdrivers, and fruity drinks served with flowers and straws complete the holiday ritual. Wines, mainly from Europe and Australia, are widely available at upmarket restaurants. Q Bar has a dedicated vodka storage room and several signature martini variations.

BEST FOR SUNSET COCKTAILS
> Cliff Bar & Grill (Lamai; p58)
> West coast resorts (West coast; p79)
> Ark Bar (Chaweng; p49)

BEST FOR LATE NIGHTS
> Green Mango (Chaweng; p51)
> Club Solo (Chaweng; p51)
> Q Bar Samui (Chaweng; p52)

Top Left Pose for a picture with some oh-so-elegant ladyboys (p110)

GREEN SAMUI

For an island that makes its living off of its natural beauty, Samui has developed so rapidly that few wild places are left and the island's resources can hardly bear the strains of the increased population of tourists and service-industry workers. The hotels are the biggest consumers, drinking more than 90% of the island's water and throwing away more than every Samui household combined.

Further complicating the environmental strain is the island's poorly developed infrastructure. The island still functions like a small village with an incinerator that has reached capacity, insufficient waste-treatment systems and limited clean water supplies. For more information on Samui's infrastructure, see p126.

One eco-leader is Sila Evason Hideaway & Spa. The hotel has a smaller footprint than most thanks to its low-key design and its day-to-day operations. Residing on a distant promontory, the hotel is more aware of its resources and excesses. It recycles its trash, uses grey water (treated water from laundry and showers) on the grounds and has its own reed-bed waste-treatment plant. The hotel has also developed a biodiesel plant that turns old cooking oil and dry coconuts into fuel that is used to power the on-site vehicles.

Tongsai Bay also adheres to a green mandate. Its grounds are designated an ecological sanctuary, and are home to 50 kinds of birds and animals. No chemicals are used on the grounds, plastics are recycled and paper bags are used instead of plastic.

Other hotels on the island fill in where the municipal infrastructure is lacking with varying degrees of environmental consideration. Though all have the best intentions, the hotels' commitments to reducing, reusing and recycling is inconsistent, and few sit at the forefront of progressive environmental sensitivity.

However, the hotels are quick to cater to the latest trends in creature comforts: from pool villas to pillow menus. Couldn't the guests desire a certain amount of ecofriendliness alongside their expectations for service and standards? For tourists in Samui to drive change, first they should be informed about what is consumed and disposed of and the pressures that these put on the environment and the infrastructure of a developing country.

When choosing a hotel, consider its conservation efforts as well as its price, location and décor. Does the hotel recycle cans, bottles and organic matter? Provide complimentary water in refundable glass bottles? Allow guests to skip daily changing of bed linen and towels? Use grey water to irrigate the property? How conscientious and developed is the hotel's sewage treatment facility? Does the hotel use solar energy for hot water?

The final step is to recalibrate your consumption habits (while still enjoying your holiday). Most guests to Thailand are conservation-minded for a Western-standard of living, which uses more resources than the old-fashioned village life that proliferated on Samui before the advent of tourism. In those bygone days, when the population was smaller, Samui had plenty of water, turtles used to visit the shores of Chaweng, and island critics predicted that rubbish would have to be imported to keep the incinerator busy. Oh how times have changed.

To lighten your environmental load, try living like a villager in a few ways: adjust the air-conditioning thermostat a few degrees warmer, flush every other trip to the toilet, use biodegradable soap to reduce water pollution. Be considerate of water usage in the shower and the sink. Dispose of plastic packaging before leaving home so that it doesn't end up in a Samui rubbish bin or worse, in the ocean. Remember to dispose of cigarette butts in rubbish bins – not on the beach. And skip the jet skis, which cause noise and water pollution, and have been accused of chasing away the turtles from Samui.

Top left Indulge your body and mind at Sila Evason Hideaway Spa (p94)

BEACHES

If you tire of the spit of sand outside your door, Samui is small enough to beach-hop with ease, earning an honorary degree in sand and sea.

Chaweng is the longest strip and has many personalities: the northern area is rocky but subdued; the central area is crowded and festive; and the southern area and the small cove of Chaweng Noi are a respite from too many bathing beauties. Further south, Lamai has some of the same tropical assets as Chaweng but on a smaller scale. Central Lamai is best for swimming, and southern Lamai is dotted with elephant-sized boulders.

Winds from the northeast cause high seas all along the east coast from December to April, and riptides can make swimming in Chaweng and Lamai dangerous, even for strong swimmers. The seas are most peaceful from July to October.

The west coast boasts Taling Ngam and Lipa Noi, two pleasant swimming beaches for day-trippers from other parts of the island.

Mae Nam is the best swimming beach in the north coast. The golden sand is soft and it is sheltered from high winds. The beach is steeply pitched, making the plunge a little abrupt for young swimmers. Bo Phut eases more gently into the sea but the sand is coarse and the water murky.

In the northeast corner, Ao Thong Sai is a real beauty with a deep cove, lush greenery and easygoing ambience. Swimming is good here but keep an eye out for submerged rocks.

Work up an appetite or thirst by strolling along the beach at Lamai (p54)

FOOD

Samui benefits from its proximity to the sea and from the culinary cross-roads that have shaped southern Thai cuisine. Malay, Indian, Chinese and Indonesian ingredients and dishes have migrated to southern Thailand, often improving the homeland's contributions.

Southern-style curries are spicier than those found in central Thailand and are typically spiked with turmeric, which imparts a yellowish hue. Fish is a common curry component as are roots and shoots that have no English-language counterparts. If your curry has broccoli and cauliflower then the cook is catering to your culture not your palate.

Cloves, cinnamon and cardamom are a few of the coveted spices of Indonesia and India that play an aromatic role in southern Thai dishes: *gaang mát·sà·mân* (Muslim curry) and *kôw mòk gài* (chicken biryani). The breakfast staple of *kà·nŏm jeen* claims Chinese heritage but tastes as if it snuck across the border from Malaysia. The pearly white rice noodles are doused with a fishy, coconut-milk sauce called *nám yah*. A signature accoutrement of southern curries and *kà·nŏm jeen* are fresh and pickled vegetables added to the dish to enhance flavour, aid digestion and temper spiciness. The southerners have even developed their own variation of *nám ʉ̃lah prík* (chilli and fish sauce) that is thick and pungent like a Malay sambal.

Samui's signature crop, the coconut, factors into almost every dish from savoury to sweet. *Wai kôo·a* is a Samui invention, using a local octopus in a spicy and sour coconut-based curry. The local catch of fresh fish and farm-raised prawns get southernised with tamarind and chilli sauces and barbecued over coals made from coconut husks.

For more on where to eat in Samui, see p12.

Search for, and then feast on, fresh seafood along the beach at Chaweng (p44)

HEALTH RETREATS & SPAS

For pampering or weight loss, Samui offers some of the world's best variety of spas and health retreats, employing Thai, Ayurvedic and Chinese traditional medicine as well as alternative medicine techniques.

Start your beach recovery with a beach massage, where you'll be pulled, kneaded and stretched into putty according to the principles of traditional Thai massage, a passive form of yoga.

For the full spa experience of being steamed, soaked and scrubbed, the hotel and day spas oblige in a setting that overlooks the sea or is tucked into the jungle. There is the usual menu of imported massage and bath products, but to 'spa locally' many places offer locally produced coconut scrubs and massage oils as well as Thai massage and the curious *bràkóp* massage (in which a heated herbal compress is pressed into acupressure points). Steam rooms are scented with a combination of Thai herbs, including lemongrass and *plai* (a type of ginger). For a post beach pick-me-up, try a foot massage based on the principles of reflexology.

But the beauty spas are *soooo* last century – today's health-trippers want rejuvenation from the inside out and are willing to work for it. Samui's health retreats have a full regimen of cleansing fasts coupled with body work, yoga, meditation, chi gung and massage. The health retreats also educate their clients in raw food cooking and self-help topics with guest lecturers. For folks who never leave home without their yoga mats, the island has intensive yoga retreats and drop-in studios. Several yoga retreats also offer teacher training classes – the best career-development excuse for a beach holiday.

For more on health retreats, yoga centres and detox programs on Samui, see p16.

BEST DAY SPAS
> Tamarind Springs (p19)
> Hideaway Spa (p94)
> Spa at Four Seasons (p82)
> Anantara Spa (p87)

BEST HEALTH RETREATS
> Spa Samui (p56)
> Kamalaya Koh Samui (p69)
> Absolute Sanctuary (p93)
> Health Oasis Resort (p82)

JUNGLE SAMUI

Take a break from the beach with an exploration of Samui's forested interior. The undulating landscape of mountains and trees swells and dips much like the ocean beyond. Waterfalls careen and cascade through the exposed rocks and collect into shallow pools before continuing to the sea. The tallest fixtures in the interior are the tree tops, not buildings, and the roads are often rutted and dusty. Most visitors do a one-day jungle safari that includes elephant trekking, 4WD tours and more attractions than you knew you liked. If the 4WD tours seem like the inland version of jet skis then embrace the idea that less is more. Opt for a less vocal exploration with a bike tour or take a vehicle to one of the accessible waterfalls for a short hike. Or you can fly, rather than walk, through the jungle on one of the island's zip-line courses. The interior also has the greatest concentration of local Samui people *(chow sà·mŭi)*, who make their living the old-fashioned way with coconut and small-scale farming. There are a variety of 'Living Thailand' tours that include buffalo shows, rice-planting demonstrations as well as elephant trekking and waterfall spotting.

BEST JUNGLE SITES
> Nam Tok Na Muang 2 (p67)
> Nam Tok Wang Saotong (p68)
> Magic Garden (p67)

BEST JUNGLE ACTIVITIES
> Waterfall Jungle Treks (p69; pictured above)
> Canopy Adventures (p41)

SNAPSHOTS

KO SAMUI FOR KIDS

The beach is always a blast for children but Thailand doubles the fun. Thais love children, especially babies, and will go out of their way to shower them with attention. *Já ăir* is Thai for 'peekaboo', and even the grumpy taxi drivers know this smile-inducing game.

The best beaches for families with young children are Bo Phut and Mae Nam. The waves are gentle, the footpaths wide enough to push a stroller, and there are other families to provide international playmates. Bring an umbrella stroller because the footpaths are crowded and curbs rarely have cutaways. If using a baby backpack, make sure the child's head doesn't sit higher than yours: there are lots of hanging obstacles poised at a forehead level. Disposable nappies in big sizes are available at Samui's Tesco Lotus and Tops Market.

For families with older children, especially teenagers, Chaweng will provide the most entertainment. The waves are powerful, there's plenty of shopping and eating, and most hotels have pools for swimming diversity.

There are lots of kid-oriented animal shows, such as monkey theatres and tiger zoos, that rarely live up to Western standards of animal welfare. Instead, head to the south coast, where kids can ride elephants to jungle waterfalls (p69) or chase butterflies in the Samui Butterfly Garden (p68).

Nearby Ko Pha-Ngan (p98) has a reputation as a party island, but there are plenty of family-friendly spots. To explore the underwater landscape, take a trip to Ko Tao (p101).

Spy on the majestic butterflies at Samui Butterfly Garden (p68)

SHOPPING

One upshot of Samui's upward mobility is the overall improvement of shopping on the island. Clothing boutiques in Chaweng and Fisherman's Village offer more than just the rayon faràng sarongs and the Beer Chang T-shirts that you find in most beach shops. For women, Chaweng shares a closet with Bali, India, Bangkok and Hong Kong. The dresses are cute and flirty, perfect for a tropical setting and its humid temperatures. A few shops in Chaweng also sell dresses for your return to civilisation with designer labels or club-worthy couture. In Fisherman's Village, the boutiques are more in tune with the 'earth mamas' and offer Chiang Mai–made natural cotton outfits that pass as outdoor wear but feel as cosy as pyjamas.

Beyond the factory-issue souvenirs, Chaweng also specialises in décor memories. The copy artists can render (or more bluntly put, rip off) any artist's masterpiece into an oil canvas all your own. You might not have had time to survey Bangkok's burgeoning design craze, but a few shops in Chaweng sell stand-out pieces that would put you in the pages of *Wallpaper** – the Thai version.

Also keep an eye out for Samui's most famous export, the coconut, and the many health and beauty products made from it. Pharmacies and sundry shops across the island sell coconut oil, a natural skin moisturiser. Virgin coconut oil is also a hot superfood, often touted as a better cooking oil than olive or vegetable oils.

BEST DRESSED
> Chandra (p42)
> Siddharta (p88)
> Vanities (p44)

BEST FOR DÉCOR
> Doodee Décor (p43)
> Paraphernalia (p43)
> About Art & Craft Café (p77)

TEMPLES & SHRINES

The majority of Samui's population is Theravada Buddhist and the island is sprinkled with temples venerated for their architecture, famous abbots or contemplative settings. Many tourists might weave some temple-spotting into a day's excursion, but it is difficult to understand the role of these buildings in religious life unless a visit coincides with a holy day or temple fair. Because Buddhists don't have one prescribed day of worship, the temples are always open to the faithful who come to make merit, by lighting joss sticks and offering lotus blossoms (the symbol of enlightenment) before the temple's principal Buddha figure. But the opportunity to make merit is not confined to the walls of the temple. Throughout Samui, you'll see small decorative houses on pedestals with offerings of fruit and incense. These are spirit houses, an animistic tradition that gives a comfortable dwelling place for a site's earthly guardian. Taxis also have dashboard altars, decorated with flower garlands and pictures of revered monks.

BEST TEMPLES
> Wat Khunaram (p68)
> Wat Phra Yai (p93)
> Wat Plai Laem (p93)

BEST SHRINES
> Meditation Cave (p67)
> Chedi Laem Saw (p66; pictured above)
> Spirit house at the Chaweng public beach access (p41)

>BACKGROUND

Explore the Muslim fishing village of Ban Hua Thanon (p66)

BACKGROUND

HISTORY

Very little of Samui's early history was recorded and what exists today is mainly oral history told by the older generation. The concept of 'ancient' times typically refers to 100 years ago at most, and anything that pre-dates the surviving generations' memories is lost, forgotten or otherwise uneventful.

Samui didn't start playing a role in regional or international circles until the latter half of the 20th century. Prior to this, the island was populated, as the oral stories go, by two families originally from Nakhon Si Tham-marat and a few more traders from southern China and Muslims from the Malay peninsula. The inhabitants lived off the land and sea, isolated from the mainland by an arduous ocean journey and from each other on the island due to mountainous terrain and no paved roads. It is believed that the island derives its name from the Chinese word for 'safe haven', though little historical evidence exists to confirm or deny it.

Coconut plantations, which flourished in the interior mountains, provided the first cash crop for the island and began to fuse Samui to the world at large. Coconut-shipping boats would make the journey between the mainland and the island and introduced the need for more large-scale development. In the late 1960s a village headman lobbied the central government to build a road on the island – a construction project that initially relied solely on manual labour but had to import heavy equipment from the mainland to grade high-terrain. Because there are no bridges to the mainland, the task of transporting earth-movers from the boat to the shore proved more difficult than road construction. The double-lane Ring Rd (Rd 4169) was completed in 1973, circumnavigating the island.

The other dramatic event in the island's history was the arrival of foreign tourists. Many claim the coveted title of being first, but the agreed version is that a Peace Corps volunteer arrived in the early 1970s aboard a coconut-trading boat. Lamai, and later Chaweng, became the stuff of legends for the young backpackers on the Asian hippie trail. The white sand beaches, gentle island life and easy access to marijuana made Samui the queen of the counterculture for the next 15 to 20 years.

But the island was much too pretty to be claimed by the penny pinchers for long. The Samui airport was built by Bangkok Airways in

1989 and small-scale family guesthouses started to go upmarket in search of package tourists. Samui's first luxury hotel was the Tongsai Bay, built in Choeng Mon by Akorn Hoontrakul and his Imperial Group, a Bangkok investment company, in the late 1980s. By the late 1990s, Chaweng's guesthouses had converted themselves into hotel resorts.

Following the 2004 Indian Ocean tsunami on the Andaman coast, tourism was diverted to Samui creating more demand for rooms and a market for more affluent visitors. What was already a busy tourism economy exploded with new properties to meet perceived demands. Samui's hotels continue to upgrade and foreign hotel brands are beginning to infiltrate what was mainly the locals' domain. There are more than a dozen proposals to build four- and five-star hotels between 2008 and 2010.

Samui is also becoming a retirement destination for Western baby boomers. Technically foreigners can't own land in Thailand, but there are many loopholes, including 30-year land leases and ownership of the structure placed on it. Because coastal land has become quite scarce, many foreigners looking to 'buy' have migrated into the mountainous interior where most of the local Samui population lives. Samui is often described as a fried egg: the whites are on the outside and the locals are in the middle yolk. The influx of newcomers moving into the mountains has caused tensions with locals over contested land ownership, forest destruction and the flooding caused by denuded hill-sides. But for some Samui people, the real-estate boom has transformed their lives from subsistence to middle class.

In many ways Samui has been very lucky, just as the price of coconuts as a commodity was beginning to decline, tourism came along as a replacement 'crop'. And just as the island was beginning to lose its lustre amongst the fickle beachgoers, the tsunami brought an unexpected boon to business, allowing the island to upgrade its image. With Phuket and the Andaman beaches back online, will Samui be too zealous in its attempts to keep the tourist numbers up? Some worry this is the case, but this island has always landed on the right side of fortune.

SHOW ME THE MONEY
About 10,000B is an average monthly salary for a Samui taxi driver. This is the starting price of one night at many of Samui's luxury hotels. If the driver is unmarried, he might send about half of the monthly salary home to support his parents.

LIFE AS A SAMUI RESIDENT

The great technological advancements of the island have occurred within most residents' lifetime. Those 50 years old and older can recall when travel between Chaweng and Lamai was done by foot, when the first TV arrived and when they saw the first motorcycle. Development has occurred at warp speed: going from a subsistence culture to a modern tourist economy in about 35 years.

Before tourism, the families who had the means sent their children to Bangkok for an education or for job training. Because the journey took days, few returned and those who did often had failed in the big city. But the arrival of tourism gave Samui exiles a reason to return and many families who had previously made a modest living fishing or raising coconuts became the island's aristocrats thanks to successful hotel operations or real-estate deals. Though Samui often feels very international, the local families still manage almost all aspects of the island, from the hotel groups to the jet-ski cartels. And though locals complain that Samui has become too busy and crowded, many remain on the island because there are job opportunities and because of the strong bonds of family.

Many sources claim that Samui people *(chow sà·mŭi)* have their own unique identity, distinct from the mainland, but the former generation's Diaspora to Bangkok and their subsequent return has imported a national identity, typically referred to as Bangkok culture. In the local areas of the interior, there is a more distinctive island culture: the older generation still speaks *pah·săh 'bàk đâi*, the southern Thai dialect, and some families still live a simple life off of the land. Like many parts of Thailand that have developed quickly, the old ways of picking breakfast from the garden orchard and fishing for dinner from the sea is much revered and often remembered as a time free from trouble. Those who have not joined the island elite are caught in the modern age with antique skills. The fisherfolk might be experts of the seas but their one-man operations don't fetch enough to afford modern life: motorcycles, refrigerators and an education. Others have faired quite well with the transition, trading a modest wooden shack for a two-storey modern house and sending their children to the mainland for an education.

Further jumbling the island's identity is the influx of Thai workers from the mainland, especially from southern and northeastern (Isan) Thailand. Regional prosperity differences often translate into segregation within the workforce: the hotel managers tend to be from Bangkok, the

HELLO MISTER

When you venture into places where few Westerners have tread, there is usually a gang of local kids bold enough to escort you from place to place and shower you with 'Hello Misters'. Ever wondered what would happen to these kids once they grew up? If they are lucky, they would become successful, well-educated businesspeople, like Ruengnam Chaikwang, a Samui native who is the director of Montien House Resort in Chaweng. As a kid growing up in Lamai, he remembers following the backpackers around and trying out English phrases. He later earned a degree in civil engineering and worked in the US for four years before returning to his native island to join in the burgeoning tourism industry. He has run unsuccessfully for mayor but continues to play a role in the management of the island as president of the Thai Hotels Association.

housekeepers from Isan. Throughout Thailand, people from the impoverished area of Isan have been the muscle behind the machine. They are the construction workers who saw and hammer in sandals and virtual ski-masks to protect against the sun. Unheard of on Samui 20 years ago, Isaners have brought their regional dish of *sôm đam* and *kôw něe-o,* both evocative of landlocked rice-planting landscape to this coastal setting.

GOVERNMENT & POLITICS

Although Samui is 250 sq km, which is approximately equivalent to Penang, Malaysia, the island is classified as a *têt-sà-bahn* (municipality), a designation based on its full-time population of about 45,000 people. It is one of the largest municipalities in Thailand and it hosts 1.5 million tourists every year, as well as unregistered labourers and other part-time inhabitants.

Unlike Phuket, which is its own province and controls its own provincial budget, Samui shares more than half of its revenues with the province of Surat Thani and has no dedicated voice in the national parliament. Due to this bureaucratic quirk and a municipal government that has been criticised for 'being asleep', Samui's infrastructure has not kept up with development.

Some first-time visitors to Thailand might think that the country is unable to build modern functioning cities, but Samui is an extreme example of government failure. Once a marvel for the island, Samui's primary highway, the Ring Rd, is in need of repairs and even a little beautification. Locals often point out that the provincial capital of Surat Thani has

beautifully maintained roads, voicing a common perception that the
mainland is unfairly siphoning off funds, though the funding for such
capital improvements comes from the national department of transport
not from the provincial government.

Samui is in the midst of developing a comprehensive plan to improve
energy production, water collection and distribution, and waste treatment and removal. If the plan is accepted, the next hurdles are imple-
mentation and funding. In the meantime, most hotels compensate
with their own generators and waste-treatment processes because the
municipal services are inefficient and unreliable.

ENVIRONMENT

Samui is the largest island in the Gulf of Thailand and sits 35km from
the mainland port of Surat Thani. The exterior of the island is ringed by
beaches and the interior is mountainous, reaching an altitude of 635m at
Khao Taay Kwai. About half of the mountainous area is covered by
deciduous forests or coconut trees and the island's primary rivers and
water sources originate from these peaks.

Samui has lost most of its coastal forest cover due to hotel construction, and residential development is moving inland to the mountains.
The offshore reefs, which are feeding grounds for fish and other marine
life, were badly damaged or completely killed off by the 1998 El Niño
phenomenon, in which ocean temperatures rose for a prolonged period.

Inviting so many tourists to play in this tropical sandbox, Samui has
struggled to house, feed and clean up after its guests. It is estimated that
Samui generates between 140 and 120 tonnes of solid waste a day with
hotels being the biggest culprits. The island's incinerator is already at

capacity and, at the current rate of growth, the island's daily waste output will increase by more than five times in 10 years.

Studies have found that the garbage crisis is solvable with increased recycling efforts. Currently only 2% of waste is recycled, but this could be increased to 15% to 20% by separating out food waste and recyclable cans and bottles. And recycling is a profitable business: hotel employees can earn extra money by selling recyclables to collectors and businesses can sell organic waste to biogas plants on the mainland.

The island's water supply is in a pinch too. Samui gets most of its water from the seasonal monsoon rains, mainly from October to December. Excess supplies are stored and used throughout the dry season. One landmark reservoir is Chaweng Lake but due to surrounding development and pollution, the water doesn't meet safety standards and is used only in cases of water shortage.

The business sector is responsible for 90% of the island's water consumption, while households account for only 10%. According to studies, the island's water capacity (including reservoirs and mountain rivers) can handle 11,000 rooms, a number that has already been surpassed and will probably reach 20,000 rooms by the end of 2008.

Treating and disposing of sewerage is another critical problem for the island. The municipal waste-treatment plant in Chaweng wasn't functional at the time of writing and has been accused of not properly treating sewage before discharging it into the waste-water canals. Most hotels deal with waste in a variety of ways. Some, like Sila Evason Hideaway and Coral Bay Resort, have model treatment methods that involve several stages of filtration. Other hotels partially treat the waste water through basic septic systems, and others flush it directly out to sea with minimal neutralisation.

The island needs critical infrastructure, all of which can be bought with time and money. To its credit, the island's environmental issues are relatively minor compared with the long-lasting pollution from industrial manufacturing.

FURTHER READING

Samui has not been much of a literary muse, but it did garner a role in Alex Garland's *The Beach,* about a secret commune in a Thai island paradise. The main characters travelled through the 'beaten path' of Samui to reach the fabled village – allegedly an island in the Ang Thong National

TUNE IN
Samui Channel (channel 10; www.samuichannel.tv) is a Samui-based TV station that features locally produced programs about local events, environmental issues and interviews with Samui folks. Check out its website for a preview of its daily programming.

Park – where peace, love and sunbathing ruled. When it came time to film the movie, producers chose Ko Phi-Phi and Phuket as stand-ins.

Except for guidebooks, very little historical and cultural information about the island exists. An upcoming academic paper on the island's ethnohistory is being compiled by Yuthasak Chatkaewnapanon, a PhD candidate in the department of tourism at University of Otago in Dunedin, New Zealand.

Otherwise, we recommend reading *Culture Shock: Thailand,* by Robert and Nanthapa Cooper, which explains Thailand's quirky, curious and practical customs.

DIRECTORY
TRANSPORT
ARRIVAL & DEPARTURE
AIR

Samui's airport is located in the northeast of the island near Big Buddha Beach. The monopoly that Bangkok Airways had on flights into and out of Samui ended in early 2008, and Thai Airways International has begun a Samui–Bangkok service. Other airlines are expected to follow.

Bangkok Airways (www.bangkokair .com) operates flights roughly every 30 minutes between Samui and Bangkok (2000B to 4000B, one to 1½ hours). **Thai Airways** (☎ in Bangkok 0 2134 5403; www.thaiair.com) operates between Samui and Bangkok (5600B, twice a day). Both airlines land at Bangkok's Suvarnabhumi Airport.

There is a **Bangkok Airways** (☎ 0 7742 0512-9) office in Chaweng and another at the **airport** (☎ 0 7742 5011). The first (at 6am) and last (9pm) flights of the day are always the cheapest.

Bangkok Air also flies from Samui to Phuket (2000B to 3000B, one hour, three daily), Pattaya (3000B, one hour, three daily), Krabi (1600B, one hour, three times a week) and Chiang Mai (4500B to 6500B, 2½hours, twice a week). International flights go directly from Samui to Singapore (4200B to 5400B, three hours, daily) and Hong Kong (6000B to 12,000B, four hours, five days a week).

During the high season, make your flight reservations far in advance as seats do sell out. If Samui flights are full, try flying into Surat Thani from Bangkok and taking a short ferry ride to Samui. Flights to Surat Thani are

ALTERNATIVE TRANSPORT OPTIONS

If you're unable to book a flight directly to Samui or want an alternative to the fuel-guzzling planes, Samui can be reached via the mainland town of Surat Thani by boat. To reach Surat Thani catch a bus from Bangkok's southern bus terminal (from 500B, 10 hours). And then take a ferry to Samui (200B, three hours) to the island.

Surat Thani is also on the train line and is an overnight journey from Bangkok. Sleeping berths start at 500B. Travel agents sell a variety of train/bus-boat combinations that can be arranged online or in Bangkok, but do be aware that agents promise and charge for more than what is delivered. The most benign scams might be an advertisement for VIP service that turns out to be run-of-the-mill ordinary.

generally cheaper than a direct flight to the island.

Ko Samui Airport

Check with your hotel for complimentary airport transfer. Otherwise, the airport minibus has affordable door-to-door service to the beach hotels. Taxis typically charge 300B to 500B for airport transfer. Some Chaweng travel agencies arrange minibus taxis for less.

VISAS

Residents of Australia, Canada, New Zealand, South Africa, the UK and the USA can stay in Thailand for 30 days without a visa. See the website of the **Ministry of Foreign Affairs** (www.mfa.go.th) for more information.

RETURN/ONWARD TICKET

Technically, you're supposed to demonstrate proof of a return or onward ticket on arrival; however, in practice, you are unlikely to be asked to show it.

DEPARTURE TAX

International travellers have to pay a separate 500B departure tax after checking in at the Samui airline counter.

GATEWAY CITIES
Surat Thani

If you're unable to book a flight directly to Samui, the mainland town of Surat Thani has an airport with service to Bangkok. **Thai Airways International** (www.thaiair.com) and **Air Asia** (www.airasia.com) fly daily from Bangkok to Surat Thani (3000B to 3200B). The Surat airport is located in the Phunphin district, 20km west of the city. From Surat you can take a boat to the island (see the boxed text, p129).

Bangkok

Most international visitors will arrive in Bangkok first and then continue on another flight to Samui. It is recommended you overnight in Bangkok in both directions to accommodate potential plane delays or cancellations. All international and Samui-bound flights leave from Bangkok's Suvarnabhumi Airport. Metered taxis from the airport to the city should cost from about 200B to 300B, plus a 50B airport departure surcharge and roughly 60B in tolls. Non-metered taxis are available but always counter-offer by halving their original offer. There is no longer a separate international departure tax levied on passengers leaving Suvarnabhumi Airport. **Novotel Suvarnabhumi Airport** (☎ 0 2131 1111; www.novotel.com; r 4500–6000B) is within walking distance of the airport and has day-use rates. Otherwise, central Bangkok is 30 minutes away, depending on traffic.

CLIMATE CHANGE & TRAVEL

Travel – especially air travel – is a significant contributor to global climate change. At Lonely Planet, we believe that all travellers have a responsibility to limit their personal impact. As a result, we have teamed with Rough Guides and other concerned industry partners to support Climate Care, which allows travellers to offset the greenhouse gases they are responsible for with contributions to energy-saving projects and other climate-friendly initiatives in the developing world. Lonely Planet offsets all staff and author travel.

For more information, turn to the responsible travel pages on www.lonelyplanet. com. For details on offsetting your carbon emissions and a carbon calculator, go to www.climatecare.org.

GETTING AROUND

Samui isn't a large island but it is difficult to get around because of traffic, poor road conditions and expensive taxis. In this book, the icon 🚐 indicates that the site is accessible via sŏrng·tăa·ou (often written 'sawngthaew'), Samui's version of public transportation.

SŎRNG·TĂA·OU

The public red sŏrng·tăa·ou (a converted pick-up truck with two benches in the back for seating) circumnavigate the island via the Ring Rd (Rd 4169) from 6am to 6pm. Some sŏrng·tăa·ou deviate from the Ring Rd to Lamai Beach Rd and to Chaweng Beach Rd. During the day, trips within one beach area (say, within Chaweng) cost 20B and trips between beaches (Chaweng to Lamai) cost 30B. No trip should cost more than 60B. After dark, the sŏrng·tăa·ou can be chartered for a negotiated fee.

The sŏrng·tăa·ou have a set route but no designated stops. You stand on the side of the road and wave them down (wave with your palm facing the ground). To disembark ring the buzzer and pay the driver. Make sure you have small bills or exact change.

TAXI

Taxis are widespread on the island but they are expensive, often matching prices in New York City. All taxis are outfitted with, and are required to use, meters but drivers never turn them on for a variety of reasons. Some drivers explain that the competition for customers is so high that they can't clear their daily vehicle rent (1000B) if they use the meters, but others know that price collusion and strong-arm tactics keep the meters turned off. This means that taxi customers must bargain for a price before boarding, which introduces the possibility of being ripped off.

To avoid bargaining nightmares, many hotels and businesses offer their own transfer services. But in general, taxi drivers are decent folks trying to make a living and as long as you agree on a price beforehand you'll be delivered without incident. If you find a taxi driver you trust, ask for their business card and call them for advance pick-ups.

Most trips within a beach area cost from 100B to 200B, within a coastal area they are 300B, and between coasts cost from 300B to 400B. You shouldn't pay more than 500B for one trip.

Motorcycle taxis can be found along the beach roads in Chaweng and Lamai. They charge about half what a taxi would charge, but you also must bargain.

CAR & MOTORCYCLE

If the roads were in better condition, renting a private vehicle would be the best option for getting around the island. Rental cars (from 1500B per day) and motorcycles (200B per day) are cheaper than taxis and allow you the freedom to roam. But driving patterns are more erratic here than elsewhere in Thailand and the roads are too small to accommodate the traffic.

Thailand follows the British custom of driving on the left, a technicality few drivers adhere to.

People drive in every which direction (not always the assigned one). The oncoming lane and shoulder is often used as a passing lane regardless of approaching clearance. Remember that in Thailand, the bigger vehicle always has the right-of-way regardless of distance or safety. The shoulder is typically for slower traffic, like motorcyclists, and larger vehicles will expect motorcycles to get out of the way.

Travel agencies, guesthouses and some hotels rent cars and motorcycles. Check the vehicle with the agent and point out any existing dents or marks to avoid charges after your return. Don't leave your passport as collateral.

BOAT

Samui is accessible by boat from the mainland port town of Surat Thani and from Ko Pha-Ngan (with service on to Ko Tao). There are seven piers on the island but most tourists will only need to know about three. The pier in Na Thon has the most options with service to Surat Thani (110B to 190B, one to three hours), Ko Pha-Ngan (130B to 250B, 20 minutes to one hour) and on to Ko Tao (350B to 600B, one to 2½ hours). Most people who stay in Chaweng use the pier at Big Buddha Beach for trips to Ko Pha-Ngan and Ko Tao. Mae Nam, on the north coast, also has passenger service to Ko Pha-Ngan and Ko Tao. Prices vary depending on the type of boat rather than the pier.

PRACTICALITIES

BUSINESS HOURS

Samui operates on 'island' time: most businesses don't open until 10am and close around 6pm. Chaweng is the night owl, with businesses operating from 11am or noon to 11pm or midnight. Banks are open Monday to Friday from 8.30am to 3.30pm; some keep weekend hours.

ELECTRICITY

Electric currents in Thailand are 220V, 50 cycles. Most electrical wall outlets take the round, two-prong terminals, but some will take the three-pronged ones. Converters can be easily bought from vendors in Chaweng.

EMERGENCIES

If you have something stolen or need assistance from the police, call the **Tourist Police** (☎ 0 7742 1281).

Samui's private hospitals have international standards and should be contacted directly if there is a medical emergency.
Bangkok Hospital (☎ 0 7742 9555; Taweerat Phakdee Rd, Chaweng)
Samui International Hospital (☎ 0 7723 0781; Chaweng Beach Rd, North Chaweng)

The seas of Samui can be rough, even for strong swimmers and drownings do occur, especially in Chaweng and Lamai, which experience strong currents and riptides. See the boxed text, p56, for tips on surviving a riptide.

HOLIDAYS

Lunar holidays change each year; check out the website of the **Tourism Authority of Thailand** (TAT; www .tatnews.org).
New Year's Day 1 January
Magha Puja Lunar holiday in February or March.
Chakri Day 6 April
Songkran 13 to 15 April
Coronation Day 5 May
Visakha Puja Lunar holiday in May
Asalha Puja Lunar holiday in July
Khao Phansa Lunar holiday in July
Queen's Birthday 12 August
Chulalongkorn Day 23 October
King's Birthday 5 December
Constitution Day 10 December

INTERNET

Internet access is widespread, if a little slow, and usually costs 2B per minute. Wi-fi is available on the island through hotspots at various hotels, cafés and restaurants. These sites are helpful for trip planning and island news:
Camille's Samui Weather (samui-weather .blogspot.com) Samui resident's daily blog about the weather, restaurants and local goings-on.

DIRECTORY

Koh Samui (www.kosamui.com) Has helpful tips on the beaches, restaurants and bars.
Sawadee.com (www.samui.sawadee.com) The island's online booking site with travellers' reviews of hotels and guesthouses.

LANGUAGE

Thailand's official language is Thai. Some Samui residents speak the southern Thai dialect, which is a little faster and uses some different words than standard Thai. Thai is a tonal language, with five tones. Written Thai is read from left to right. Transliteration of Thai into the Roman alphabet renders multiple (and contradictory) spellings. After every sentence, men affix the polite particle kháp, and women khá.

BASICS

Hello.	sà·wàt·dee (kráp/kâ)
Goodbye.	lah gòrn
How are you?	sa-bai dee măi?
I'm fine, thanks.	sà·bai dee
Excuse me.	kŏr à·pai
Yes.	châi
No.	mâi châi
Thank you.	kòrp kun
You're welcome	mâi Ђen rai
Do you speak English?	kun pôot pah·săh ang·grìt dâi măi?
I (don't) understand.	(mâi) kôw jai
How much?	tôw raí?
That's too expensive.	paang geun Ђai

EATING & DRINKING

Two beers, please.	kŏr bee·a sŏrng kòo·at
This food is delicious!	ah·hăhn née a·ròy!
Please bring the bill.	kŏr bin nòy
I'm allergic to ...	pŏm/dì·chăn páa ...
I don't eat ...	pŏm/dì·chăn gin ... mâi dâi
meat	néu·a sàt
chicken	gài
fish	Ђlah

EMERGENCIES

I'm ill.	chăn Ђòo·ay
Help!	chôo·ay dôo·ay!
Call ...!	rêe·ak ... nòy!
a doctor	mŏr
the police	đam·ròo·at

DAYS & NUMBERS

today	wan née
tomorrow	prûng née
yesterday	mêu·a wahn

0	sŏon
1	nèung
2	sŏrng
3	săhm
4	sèe
5	hâh
6	hòk
7	jèt

8	ɓàat
9	gôw
10	sìp
11	sìp·èt
12	sìp·sŏrng
13	sìp·săhm
20	yêe·sìp
21	yêe·sìp·èt
22	yêe·sìp·sŏrng
30	săhm·sìp
100	nèung róy
200	sŏrng róy
1000	nèung pan

MONEY

The basic unit of Thai currency is the baht (B). Notes come in denominations of 20B, 50B, 100B, 500B and 1000B, while coins come in 1B, 5B and 10B and occasionally 25 satang or 50 satang. Go to 7-Eleven stores or other hotels to break 1000B notes.

Exchanging money, accessing money through bank ATMs and cashing travellers cheques are all easy transactions. You'll have very few problems when using your credit card – particularly if it's a Visa or MasterCard. Exchange rates can be found in the Quick Reference section in the front of this book.

Excluding lodging, which can range from 1000B to 10,000B, average daily costs will be between 2000B to 5000B, depending on your spending habits.

NEWSPAPERS & MAGAZINES

Samui has several tourist-oriented advertorial publications, including *Essential, Samui Guide, Passport, Samui Lifestyle, C-Holiday Magazine* and *Absolute Samui*. The English language newspaper is *Samui Express*.

PHOTOGRAPHY

Internet shops in Chaweng can burn CDs featuring your digital photographs.

TELEPHONE

Thailand is on a GSM network and cellular operators include AIS, Orange and DTAC – all of which allow you to use their SIM cards in some imported phones. Refill cards are widely available.

COUNTRY & CITY CODES

All Thai phone numbers start with ☎ 0 and the area code, except in the case of mobile numbers, which start with ☎ 08.
Thailand ☎ 66
Samui (land lines) ☎ 077

USEFUL PHONE NUMBERS

International Direct Dial Codes
☎ 001, ☎ 007, ☎ 008.

TIPPING

Tipping practices vary in Thailand, but many midrange and expensive restaurants add a 10% service charge to the bill in addition to a 7% VAT (value-added tax).

TOURIST INFORMATION

Samui's **TAT office** (☎ 0 7742 0504; Na Thon) is at the northern end of Na Thon and has friendly English-speaking staff and handy brochures and maps.

TRAVELLERS WITH DISABILITIES

The infrastructure in Samui is so basic that few areas and businesses are accessible. Movement around Samui can be difficult in a wheelchair: footpaths are limited, crowded and rarely have kerb cutaways.

Kŏr bee-a singh năng kŏad kráp
/ ká.

>INDEX

See also separate subindexes for Do (p142), Drink (p143), Eat (p143), Play (p143), See (p144) and Shop (p144).

000 map pages

🍸 DRINK

Bars
Ark Bar 49, 50, 110, 111
Baan Taling Ngam Resort & Spa 79
Ban Sabai Sunset Beach Resort & Spa 79
Bar Solo 49
Billabong Surf Club 91
Black Jack Pub 49-50
Easy Time Bar 50
Five Islands 79
Frog & Gecko Pub 91
Good Karma 50
Nathalie's Art Palace 50
Pier 91-2
Ruby Red Lounge 53
Samui Shamrock 63
Tropical Murphy's 50-1, 111

Clubs
Bauhaus Club 62

Lounges
Beach Republic 62-3
Nikki Beach 79
Woo Bar 84

🍴 EAT

Brazilian
Zico's 48

French
Café Aux Amis 45-6

Fusion
Betelnut 45

International
About Art & Craft Café 76, 77, 119
Akwa Restaurant 44-5
Angela's Bakery 82
BBC 94
Bophut Luck 89
Captain Kirk 46
Coast Restaurant 58-9
Coffee Junction 89
Karma Sutra 89
Kokomiko 59
Page Restaurant 47
Rocky's 61
Sapphire Blue Restaurant 53
Shack 90
Wave Samui 48
Will Wait 62-3
Zazen Restaurant 91

Italian
Alla Baia 89
Bellini 45
Prego 48
Vecchia Napoli 48
Villa Bianca 90-1

Markets
Hua Thanon Market 13, 66, 71
Laem Din Market & Night Market 13, 47
Lamai Day Market 13, 59-60
Mae Nam Market 83
Na Thon Day Market 77
Na Thon Night Market 13, 77
Plai Laem Fish Market 92

Mediterranean
Cliff Bar & Grill 58, 111

Pan-Asian
Dining on the Rocks 94

Seafood
Bang Po Seafood 13
Sabeinglae 13, 61-2

Tex-Mex
Gringo's Cantina 46-7

Thai
About Art & Craft Café 76, 77, 119
Akwa Restaurant 44-5
Bang Po Seafood 13, 83
Big John Seafood 79
Café Aux Amis 45-6
Coast Restaurant 58-9
E-San Yam Sabb 46
Go Wat 59
Hua Thanon Market 13, 66, 71
Krua Bang Po 83
Laem Din Market & Night Market 13, 47
Lamai Day Market 13, 59-60
Lamai Night Food Centre 61
Mae Nam Market 83
Malee Restaurant 89-90
Na Thon Day Market 77
Na Thon Night Market 13, 77
Nut's Restaurant 71
Page Restaurant 47
Pee Soon 47
Radiance Restaurant 61
Ran Kuaytiaw Leuk Lap 94
Sabeinglae 13, 61-2
Sojeng Kitchen 48
Srinuan Thai Food Restaurant 2 62
Starfish & Coffee 90
Uncle Noi's 84
Wave Samui 48
Will Wait 62-3
Zazen Restaurant 91

Vegetarian
Radiance Restaurant 61

⭐ PLAY

Clubs
Club Solo 51, 111
Gecko Village 26, 92, 110

INDEX

000 map pages